LESSONS IN IMPERMANENCE

A Barn-Dweller's Guide to Woodwork and Buddhism in Brittany

Jane Parry

PARTHIAN

Parthian
The Old Surgery
Napier Street
Cardigan
SA43 1ED

www.parthianbooks.com

First published in 2014

ISBN 978-1-909844636

Cover Image: Chris Iliff www.chrisiliff.co.uk
Typeset by Elaine Sharples
Printed and bound by Gomer Press, Llandysul, Wales

Published with the financial support of the Welsh Books Council

British Library Cataloguing in Publication Data

A cataloguing record for this book is available from the British Library.

"In certain alchemical tracts there are three stages described as being necessary to transformation: the *nigredo*, the black or the dark dissolving stage, the *rubedo*, the red or the sacrificial stage, and the *albedo*, the white or the resurgent stage."

Women Who Run With the Wolves – Clarissa Pinkola Estés

The Barn

August 2008

When we drove up to it, it seemed the right place. Late, October sun splashed the old stone walls. The approach was a gentle incline, past a still, dappled pond; a welcome change from hot, unrelenting fields. The Golden Hour. I should have known.

Broad oaks surrounded the long, low barn. Long and low enough that we would not need super-tall scaffolding to do the roof, I thought. Long and low, like a shoebox: manageable.

We had spent the October half-term driving down from north Wales to north Brittany, two kids in the back of the car. Anna, age 6, quietly sicked up her croissant in Rostrenen. We met agents at church squares and viewed massive edifices for sale, each too big for their English owners to manage. As we drove away from another possibility from our 100 euro 'budget', I remember thinking how pathetic a small patch of cultivated land looked – recently-planted pansies, along with the new wooden fence. The house an enormous, beastly thing, the garden an attempt to tame and anglicise the impossible hugeness of it all. The house for sale as the marriage probably ended, I thought. The wife had probably left – too much, too remote, too difficult. An old woman, sitting in the doorway, looked up as we scooted off down the dusty track, a goat by her side. Seen it all before.

At the barn, we looked at space and possibilities. The children played innocently with some balls left behind in the building, happy to be freed from the trauma of the Citröen and the endless travelling. The genial farmer walked us slowly around the land in the apple-softened light. He seemed charming, in a French, ruddy-faced, blue-shirted kind of way – *in his 70s and still looking so young!* We met his family – wife, children and grandchildren – *so many grandchildren! Look how they kiss so often!* We saw the large oaks and chestnuts that mark the perimeter of the land.

We walked the dusty track around the property, skirting the acre-patch, past a tin shed on the other side, metallic blue in the light.

'What's that?' I asked.

'The pigshed,' it was translated.

Oh, how quaint, I thought – a proper working farm for us to experience proper farmyard animals. A truly rural environment, but not too far from the neighbours.

We had tried buying a house and workshop in Wales, but it had never worked out; several sales fell through. This barn was possible – it was affordable, about a third of the price of a comparable property in Wales. We saw the large interior space, empty and wide, with beams running up to the ceiling, in the block-built section. Empty. We saw space.

Six months later, on a raw April morning, the day we were to finally sign, I stood in the oldest part of the building, on the earth floor, and cried.

'But it will mean starting from scratch!' I wept.

The wind whistled through the eaves. The lighting wire hung from the low eroded beam; a light bulb at the end gave no illumination. I stood with James in the darkened space, which the rain made dreary outside and in. I had started from scratch once before and I knew that living with bags of concrete is not easy. We had built the interior of the tall mid-terrace we currently lived in, when the children were babies. I used to get up in the morning and cry at the concrete floor. Things had progressed, but I was cautious of bare earth and breakdown potential.

We bought it. The night before, we stayed at a local hotel, one of the two in the small town that didn't look like a brothel. It was cheap, and reasonably nasty, with the thinnest of everything. The entrance from the street to our room seemed to be through a urinal, and I bleakly remember gagging on the peculiar dinner we were served that evening. Memories of the back of my nana's cupboard, with its wartime, 'just in case' tins of potatoes and peas, but these particular Brittany ones seemed to be cooked in vinegar. I politely ate several peas and covered the rest with my napkin.

We recovered a bit the next day, sitting on the green bank of the wide river. We would do it up over time, we decided. James would go backwards and forwards, me and the children would come out in the holidays. We signed, amidst the formal etiquette of the *Notaire's* office. Monsieur and Madame tenant farmer in their best clothes, our estate agent glib and slick, the *Notaire* efficient, keen that we understood the whole process. He suggested we apply for planning permission that same year, so that our files were still near the top of the pile. Handshakes all round.

We drove back to our barn. There were no keys, as there were no locked doors. We bought some tealight candles and stayed the first night on our land in a dinky tinky caravan Monsieur had given us, with authentic dinky tinky French numberplates. A particularly kind donation, I thought. A small price to pay, I guess, for the 98,000 euros we had just handed over.

We bought steak, salad and spuds, and ate them outside, before the light went. And that's when we smelt it. That particular, pervasive scent, wafted over by the change in the breeze. From the north, now. Pigshit.

Pig

Shit.

Nothing quite like it.

I couldn't believe what I was smelling. I don't think either of us could. It didn't waft our way and then waft away again. It just kept on wafting, straight at us. Suddenly, I could sense that maybe (just maybe) this was not such a glittering prize. There was a downward spiral starting, in my stomach.

God, but that caravan was cold. I woke every hour that night, with a slightly delirious-making crazy pain in my thighs. I wore everything I had, and we cuddled up some, but damn, it was cold. In the morning we washed under the outdoor tap, took many photographs of the dark interior, the lay of the stones in the facing wall – every aspect, in fact, to help us remember the extent of the place. Then we drove home to Wales. I couldn't escape the olfactory memory of pigshit.

Over the next few months James began what would become a routine of travel backwards and forwards from Wales to France. He bought a big French van. He was practical and energetic. I didn't know quite what to do with myself the first time he was away. Though he was only gone for ten days, it was the first time we had ever spent a night apart in our marriage. Me and the kids joined him at the barn in the summer holidays.

The first summer was a heatwave. People all over the country were dying – the old, the young. Every day Monsieur Le Métayer would come and tell us the news stories of the day, shaking his head, raising his hands. Our caravan was laid bare to the sun, which held the barn in its glare throughout the day. We would check the thermometer in Monsieur Le Métayer's flower bed – the pink and blue hydrangea blooms a neat border across the way. 37 degrees in the shade. We moved very slowly, Anna and I, watering the camelia and small fir we had just planted, backwards and forwards across the hard earth. We gazed in awe and with longing at Msr Le Métayer's manicured lawn, a mature oak perfect in the centre, with a swing hanging idle in the heat.

The coolest place was within the oldest part of the barn, the old stones in the thick walls saving us from the extraordinary heat. In the evening we would walk up the track and look across at the violet blue of Guénin hill. I took photographs of the landscape, hay bales cream against gold. The children ran across stubbled fields, climbing on the bales and exulting. We washed the dust off them and when they were in bed we would sit out on the hard earth in our camp-chairs, late into the night, gazing up and losing ourselves in the Milky Way, quietly amazed this place was ours.

The barn, Kersparlec, is an ancient Breton dwelling. The links between Welsh and Breton and the linguistic similarities are evident – our *Notaire* was called Pengam ('Crooked Head'), for example. 'Ker' is the prefix to many place names. The closest meaning I can find for it is 'Encampment'.

Looking at the barn from the front, the large metal doors to the modern block-built part dominate, with a ramp leading up to them. It is derelict. Agricultural. The whole area is agricultural, with ham-making factories on the motorway roads. The road up to the barn is past a small lake, big enough to row and fish in, with a magnolia tree on the bank. There is a villa with a circular tower opposite the lake, another smaller white villa on the approach. The surroundings, then, are tended.

The barn, our barn, was completely uninhabitable, so we slept in a caravan under the large and dangerous dutch barn, an enormous thing which took up most of the land. It was high, one of the metal girders was kinked, it slanted uneasily and needed pulling down.

The cousins, aunties and uncles visit, piling red out of hot cars in white cut-down trousers. Because we have no amenities at the barn, we decamp to the local campsite, with its aqua pool. There, the pale concrete surround is perfectly in keeping with the water and tanned European families. I lie back on the bleached tiles and breathe in, selfconscious in my one-piece, while the children shriek and blaze down the waterchute. I too attempt to hurtle down, but my 14 euro L'Eclerc cossie catches on the way, leaving me spluttering and snagged. It's not very sophisticated. I retreat poolside to Sartre's *Nausea* and wonder about existential angst.

I'm never quite sure if 'holiday' is the right term for this time – for James there is absolutely no question of holiday: all focus needs to be on the barn. Yet we need to spend time together, after so much time apart. So there is a confusion, because it is not wholly one thing or the other, neither full-on holiday nor full-on working mode. There is an element of frustration, a constant underlying tension, indecision over what to do with this barn and its occasional but very strong smell of pigshit. The vile smell only happens very occasionally, perhaps 85% of the time there is no sign, no hint of it.

Sometimes the kids stay over at the campsite with their aunties and uncles. They play *boules*, eat pizza and swim in the rain. Often we do a swap, and Joe and his cousin Ianto come back with me to the barn where James is demolishing the old asbestos lean-to – sweat and dust and rubble. The boys spend hours chasing lizards and winging bows and arrows. We travel about in an old red Peugeot which belches plumes of smoke and stalls a lot. People often stare in the street as we pass and sometimes I wonder why. It has out-of-town French plates, but it is as though they recognise it. Occasionally I drive on the wrong side of the road.

At the barn we cook up big meals and eat them on the long workshop table. The family walk around the land, enjoying the space and not really knowing what I am going on about when I explain about the terrible stink.

'Perhaps the pig farm will be decomissioned one day,' suggests my brother-in-law helpfully.

'These small industries must find it increasingly tough these days. In a couple of years it may be gone.'

When I was seven we lived on a smallholding – of the very makeshift kind. My mum had a young friend, Julie, who lived up in the hills above the nearby village, in a big, functional, concrete-and-tinsheds farm. Julie was married to a pigfarmer. They had two children, Trudi and Siôn. Julie was only 24 when she was diagnosed with cancer. My mum was a good friend to her through her illness and to her family after Julie died. Trudi and

Siôn were often at our house, and I knew when their dad had arrived to collect them, without having seen him.

Poor Trudi and Siôn. I should have been better to them. I should have been nicer, kinder. Quiet, unhappy children. Poor family, poor man. I wonder whether the pigshit smell has found me, whether this is Karma.

Now, two years after we bought the barn, and in this third summer, I'm sitting on the 'upper lawn' – the flat area where the filter bed for the septic tank is. It's newly grassed, and looks out west across the barley field, and back to the rear of the building. The kids are bodging around, Joe reading in the caravan and Anna pottering with sticks, steps and chairs around the plastic paddling pool. The pool has amazed us with the bright green blooms of algae that appear after only a few days. Fluorescent green, it is, the colour of joke shop slime. I expect a large primaeval monster to slither out of it.

The sky is big, here. Big and cloudy. On a good day the clouds are French dusty blue, the sort that makes you wish for a very soft chalk pastel. That's what they're like now, just not quite as romantic. The barley field is putty-coloured, a brownish cream, damp. When it is sunny, this is an obvious place to be. How could there be any question? The space and light is at its full potential, the colours at their saturated best; the blue gravel of the track, the jungle green of the high cornstalks. When it is dull, it is just that. I couldn't even be bothered to describe it as pewter, or leaden. What is the point?

At night, sometimes, when the weather is still and dull, the milky vastness gazes at me through the small hatch window of the caravan. Actually, vastness is the wrong word. The stars in their galaxy offer vastness, pinpricks of space and time – this particular light is like opaque soup. There is a closeness to it, and a terrifying feeling that all the spirits in their nightwatch have woken me. Waiting to see what I will do.

I have slept badly here. I have not slept much at all, and I have had dreams that wake me with their awfulness. I've woken with tears on my face. I've dreamt of death and more and woken shaken and been fragile all day.

Why is this? Is it because there is no noise, no streetlight, nothing to stop the mind from unravelling in its own unfettered way? I wonder about the history of this land. Have people been happy here, or is the sickle embedded in the chestnut tree a last statement of someone who was beaten by this place? Are all the people who have lived and died here still hanging around, coming out at night?

I don't think so.

At least, I think I don't think so.

There are swallows that fly in, out and around the barn. They build nests in the eaves of the workshop. Next to the workshop is the galley kitchen, separate loo and shower that James has built. These are made out of fibreboard – small, cheap and functional facilities so that he can keep clean and fed as he works. The swallows swoop over us as we mill around with cups of tea. They chatter and loop, so swiftly that if I am walking out and a swallow is on the way in, it will veer around, giving me right of way, brilliantly fast, on the threshold.

Swallows, holly, quartz. Signs of gypsy life. There were cart wheels, old vehicles and empty bottles scattered about the land when we bought it. Some of these things – like the abandoned shop van with the *Citron Pastilles* logo – had a certain charm, but they all got cleared away when we took down the massive dutch barn. The gypsies and James pulled down the sagging metal frame and dragged it away. It left a bare oil-stained patch of flat earth, which we seeded with grass and which makes a piebald lawn.

James cut down the tall, sad conifers which drooped darkly along the perimeter fence. He did this in the July heat, amidst a fury of spiteful insects that bit and stung him, even through the protective clothing. He cut back the thick, invasive ivy that was clogging the life force of the old oaks and chestnuts. They seem to breathe easier now, their trunks broad and clear against the ground and sky. He has built a wooden tree house against a chestnut, a platform in the green leaves and a plank swing.

The barn is an amalgam of three buildings, facing roughly east. The oldest part is the north end, about 500 years old. This is the side nearest the pigshed, just over the track and a traditional Breton dwelling. It has one very small barred window, a door, chimney, and earth floor. Tacked onto this is the middle section, which was lived in until about 30 years ago. It is double the size of the oldest part and has two rotten windows with a broken door inbetween. All these doors and windows are on the front side of the building. There are no windows along the back of the barn – just one door which James made, to come in and out of the workshop, kitchen and loo. This functional area is within the block-built section of the building. The building is stone throughout, apart from this modern block-built end, which forms the third and most recent section. The floor is concrete here, with metal gratings. It used to house pigs and is now full of woodworking machinery.

James works from here for five or six weeks at a time – we spend many weeks apart. He sleeps in the caravan butted up against the workshop wall, working for a new set of clients. He realises their French dream houses in the shape of staircases, windows and doors. He works continuously, designing and making for these English clients. He has a new network of French and English friends, people he's met at the French Business course. He is learning the language with commitment and enthusiasm.

When we first saw this empty space our impression was that we could have a huge open plan kitchen, with mezzanine seating area. The rafters up to the roof had a wonderful expansive symmetry, the low exterior belied the sense of scale inside. As time has gone on, the amount of compromises we've made have condensed into a wholly economical proposed design of a conventional three-bedroom house, with the workshop taking up a good portion of the space.

When we bought the barn, although it was advertised as a *longère*, in reality it was an agricultural building, and in order to do anything to it, we had to have a planning permission. It was just over the size threshold whereby you need to have planning application signed off and approved by a registered architect. So James drew up our designs and presented them to an architect to stamp and submit.

Our architect's plans were turned down once by the planning authorities. By that time, I had simply lost heart. Back in Wales, I had bought and read books on Living and Working in France, which all said roughly the same thing – that social security contributions were high, that it was very difficult (though not impossible) to make it work. Though I wasn't entirely fazed, the influence of this reading, coupled with that bloody smell, gave me real cause for doubt.

I diverted my attention from the barn. I got a promotion at work, and threw myself into that. Money was going out, on the architect's work and a septic tank (*fosse*). I began to spend money we didn't have, sticking it on the existing mortgage, relying on the equity in our Welsh house. I began to spend money with an almost gay abandon, on clothes, flights and gadgetry. And central to all this was the unmade decision about whether we were all going to live in the barn. I was resistant, reluctant. James would not push me, but continued to go backwards and forwards, creating this new life.

After many ballpark figures in my sketchbook, I couldn't see how we could afford to make it into a house. James swiftly redesigned the whole on paper, in a grim and dark January at our Welsh kitchen table. Eventually we got planning permission. The only condition was that we remove all the beautiful terracotta roof pantiles and replace with slate.

The whole thing seems to be about compromises.

Compromises and choices. We had our tall terrace house on the market at the outset, the idea being to sell up and move here. But I bottled it and withdrew from a sale, unable to let go of job, school, familiarity. It's that decision that has plagued me, for two years. Do the benefits of moving from here to France (space) outweigh the non-benefits of staying in Wales (lack of space)? Tough call. It is a constant dilemma. James has made the move, has committed to this new life – he spends roughly 6 weeks in France without us and 5 weeks in Wales, where he feels displaced. There is tension and distance and difficulty.

Today, 7th August, it is raining hard. James has taken the kids in the van down to St Nicholas. They will cycle along the towpath, I guess. They'll get wet. I'm not feeling too good, sore throat and aching all over. It is nice to be on my own for a little while. There hasn't really been much let-up this year. The promotion means lecturing full-time.

I think partly what is wrong with me is that I feel trepidation at the task which lies ahead. It involves taking the kids back to Wales, managing our lives, going back to work and putting the house back on the market. The last one is the hardest. It has to happen, I think, finally. I am going to sell the house. I'll think about where and how we live after I've done that. Selling a house is no mean feat, but I can't afford to keep this up any more – my bank balance just slides ever further in the wrong direction.

At least if we sell the house, we will be able to buy the barn outright. That will give some psychological advantage, surely. At the moment all I am doing is paying the interest on a huge mortgage. Plus credit card and car loans. If I sell the house, I can clear those debts. I'll rent somewhere nearer to work. I should aim to get somewhere I can go home for lunch. The upheaval for the kids will be big. I shall deal with one thing at a time.

Selling the house: what needs to happen. Email Agent. Fork out £300 for the Home Information Pack. Tidy up ready for photos. Prepare to prepare the kids. I should do it when the kids are back in school, but when my year hasn't quite kicked in – early September. James will be in Wales then too. A sign will go up in the front garden. People will come to look. We may get an offer – it may be the asking price, though I doubt it. The most optimistic calculations leave us with a potential outcome of £30,000 – nowhere near what we need in order to build this barn.

I'm worn out thinking about it. Why has it proved so difficult to find a home, with a bit of land? Why, in searching for the dream, have we managed to get further away from it? How long will we manage to live apart like this, separate, each doing it alone? When will I have had enough? Will this place ever be more than a white elephant? A beautiful dream in a charming spot? How much money will building bedrooms, living room and bathroom soak up?

Moving

August 2011

Whilst James was living in the barn, establishing the workshop and making work happen, my daily routine was very different. I'd drop the kids at Breakfast Club, drive an hour over the mountains to work a full day teaching, then drive all the way back again and pick up the parental reins. It was exhausting. I developed an enormous respect for single parents. Of course, though, if you are the lone adult, apart from looking after the children, ultimately you get to make your own choices, without thought for your partner. The situation as it stood meant we had no real clarity either way – trying to sustain a marriage whilst in separate countries is complicated. As it was, our marriage was brought at times to a token five-minute phone conversation, every other day. We grew more and more separate.

He would come back sometimes with raw, cracked hands, from having been working in an unheated workshop all winter. Some phone conversations took up the span of our tension as well as the smaller details – like the morning that he found a mouse in the spindle moulder. These fragments of phonecalls highlighted our different lifestyles as I made my way through my days; organising, directing and enthusing to make 'creative' things happen with the students.

I remember watching a World Cup final with the kids, in front of the TV in the small front room, with my husband maybe witnessing the same match, but in another country. There were things that didn't feel right, but I layered so much laquer on everything that you couldn't see beneath the surface. As a kid, I remember criticising my mum for papering over the cracks. How many must I have papered over since?

Eventually, I was miserable. James had been so miserable for so long that we were held very tenuously together. The constant backwards and forwards to France to earn a living was tiring and expensive. He wanted me to go with him, but I felt I could not – that I would not be able to cope, that it did not make sense. It was stalemate. I was stuck and getting progressively sadder.

I remember standing by the toaster in the kitchen: Cook, Mother, Master, Provider, Nurturer: all of those relentless, repetitive roles, thinking, *Bea is climbing mountains, James is working in France, Ali is doing the MA. Why am I here, stood in the same place?*

I felt like an observer, rather than a participant. Much later, I told my friend Raj about that feeling. He said, 'To be a participant, you have to take chances. You did not want to take chances, you wanted security.'

And he was right. It took me a long time to figure out that security is something you can carry with you, something you can give yourself. To let the one who loves you, love you. To allow belief and faith in. Life is too short to be little.

Eventually, like a bull forced into the corner of the china shop, I put the house in Wales, finally and irrevocably, back on the market. Eventually we sold it, at the bottom of the market, in the midst of the British recession. In the meantime we had moved closer to work, to a rented house. This house was large and square, set into a hill looking out to the mountains. It had a brown Formica kitchen and brown carpet tiles in the cavernous front room. Upstairs was light and warm. It was practical, functional. I was determined I would not put down roots there, but that it would be some sort of staging post, somewhere neutral for two years, while we found a tenant and ultimately a buyer for our terrace house. I propped up paintings and even made some, but I did not hammer a nail or screw into that house. It was a transient home. There was a period where rent and mortgage were both going out. I budgeted hard.

I still hadn't committed to moving to France, but the *impasse* had become unbearable, and it was evident we couldn't carry on any more with the same unsatisfactory arrangements. James's constant travelling backwards and forwards, with the confusion and indecision causing constant tension – those miserable, staring conversations over a February kitchen table.

In the early summer of 2010, sad and confused, I sat with Raj by the sea and told him very briefly of my dilemma. He said something like, 'Who would be a carpenter in the 21st century? It is not an easy thing. If you are going to go with your husband, do it wholeheartedly, have Faith.'

And he was right. That day I went back to the brown rented house on the hill and deleted some 4000 emails. And my heart began to lift, like a kite, borne up as I decided to do the right thing, to move, to be with James, for all of us to be together, come what may.

So I tell James, as we walk around the moor by the house on the hill, and we agree a timescale: to pull myself out of work, to take the kids out of school, and to organise the process of moving, wholesale, to France.

We research French schools and write to them. Every time James goes out to the barn now he takes with him furniture and building materials: the old black piano, the brown sofa. We invest in a decent stove, a flue, and sheets of insulation, with which he will construct a 'pod-home' within the main shell of the building. I arrange to take an unpaid sabbatical from work. They will keep my job open for me for a year. I do not think I will return after that time, but it feels like a good safety net.

When we cleared out our terrace we got rid of most of the accumulated stuff. In the rented house I continue to declutter like crazy. I give away the piano keyboard, the large plastic paddling pool, certain the children have grown out of them and that we will never need them again. I feel worthy and practical, dropping these things off with friends and neighbours, with Oxfam.

Towards the end of our time in Wales, I burn the more personal stuff – diaries and photographs, in a rusty old wheelbarrow next to the elm tree on the rough land overlooking the Carneddau. I take photographs of the black and white ash, the clear flames in the bright air. The last time I had a pyre like this was about 14 years ago, just before Joe was born. It was much bigger then, it took me all afternoon to get through it – sketchbooks, mainly, that I had carried about with me through my late teens and early twenties. Oil pastel selfportraits, accounts of hitching trips to Ireland, that sort of thing.

James is working flat-out on work for French clients, plus trying to get the barn habitable for me and the kids before we go out next week.

I am moving to France.

'Oh,' they say, 'you must be so *excited!*'

Sometimes it is put as a question. 'Are you excited?'

This could provide the answer, 'No. I am not excited.' Simple. *But not what they want to hear.* They do not know; it is not their fault.

'No,' I feel like saying – though I do not. 'I am not *excited*. I am *exhausted.*'

I discover that I can smile very convincingly with big white teeth, while inside I might be breaking a little.

I think of the American author who bought a house in Italy. She described herself as wanting to be stretchered to the plane, after the end of the academic year. I imagine myself in a similar way, carried out under a starched white sheet; prone, immobile.

It seems that no matter how you try to tell them that it will be rudimentary living, basic in pretty much every way, they still seem to think that Living In France equals Living The Dream. And perhaps it is, in its way, rudimentary living or not. Certainly it is not continuing the pseudo-glossy status-quo of UK styling –

big mortgage, big loans. It is bucking the trend. But, at risk of being the Eeyore of the piece, 'excited' doesn't really capture it.

Leaving Wales was pretty grim, the house packed up and rooms left empty, family to wave us off. I was clenched up inside. We drove behind James's big white van, which was full of everything that was left of everything that we own. Anna's rabbit Mr Rufus in his hutch up close to the back door, with access for food, water and air. Mr Rufus did not die on the journey, and passed customs without comment.

I can't speak. I don't speak and neither do the children as we drive south along the motorways, carefully following the van, nose to tail. The landscape softens the further south we drive, the damp blue giving way to the lighter midlands and the rolling gold of the south. Anna's tears as we drive onto the ferry. Le Havre and sunshine, free nectarines in the corner shop – *un cadeau*: a gift.

Mr Rufus through Customs! I feel like chirpily FB-ing, but think better of it, the blithe glibness of that post seeming to tempt fate.

More driving then, through the bright, flat countryside, so vast and unfamiliar, to arrive at the barn.

Caravan

Steinbeckian: You know the beginning of *The Grapes of Wrath*, where they are walking across the land turned to dust, down at heel, impoverished, just carrying on to try to reach their destination, though that too is turned to dust? You know that bit? Well, it's like that. With a bit more dirt thrown in. Hardpacked, but it leaves a silt across every surface.

I am living in France.

There are lots of books on 'Living in France' and the lifestyle here, some of whicèh are wildly humorous, the authors being preoccupied with the difference as to whether men wink at them in Paris or London (winking being a positive, life-affirming and saucy thing). There are also books and television programmes about people who 'do up projects'. These people always have a Budget, usually in the region of around £300,000. This book isn't like that. This book has none of those things.

This book starts from scratch, with a long low building, running from north to south, facing east, its back to the west. It is what the estate agent called a *longère*. It is not a *longère* as you would know it. *Longères* have windows, and doors, with swathes of lilac wisteria trailing over blue-painted shutters. This derelict barn, while having a certain charm, needs everything doing to it. The roof has to come off, the joists need replacing, the walls need to be taken down and built back up, new foundations need to be put in. And that's before we've even begun to think about windows, doors, plastering, rendering, wiring, plumbing. All these things need to be done in order to turn it into a habitable dwelling.

Did we think of those things when we first saw it? Of course not. We saw that golden light, space and potential. But here are a few notes, in case you ever consider doing the same thing.

- Late-October sunshine softens perceptions. When the farmer tells you the shed adjacent to the barn you are viewing is 'for pigs', do not be seduced into visions of country harmony, with honking porkers merrily chowing down in the golden light. Brittany breeds pigs. We have established that pigshit stinks.
- Texturally degraded paintwork and plaster may be visually aesthetically *interesting*, within a derelict building context: this perception will diminish when you live in it.

Over the last few years we have had plenty of time to work out how much all the renovation work will cost, and thought long and hard about how we can raise the money. This can become a complicated, circuitous thinking process with a lot of dead-ends, loops and intersections.

Now we live in the barn. Actually, all four of us live in the five-berth caravan butted up alongside it. James has long since customised this caravan; in place of the original fusty old beige carpeting there is now a wooden floor. The chemical loo and tiny kitchen were ripped out and a long desk put in their place. We have our old Ulefos wood-burning stove in here, which keeps us toasty. There are framed pictures and prints on the wall, which is painted a calm blue. There is a clothes rack, book shelves, a shoe rack, two sleeping areas – all this in a roughly 16 x 7 foot space. James is a master at this sort of living. He keeps it shipshape. We sleep all in the one space, which is in its entirety much smaller than the large bedroom I had all to myself in the brown house. Joe is on a mattress on the floor, as the children are too big to share the same bed now. We sleep in the caravan and use the barn to cook, clean and eat.

Inside the barn James has begun constructing the pod-home.

He has extended the kitchen galley into a larger room, roughly 14 x 12 foot. There is a table, a sink and a stove. There are no bedrooms, there is a tiny bathroom that he is fitting upstairs, but there are no stairs yet.

On leaving Wales, I had taken a few weeks to methodically pack all our belongings – shoes in one box, winter gear in another. Cluedo, Monopoly, Scrabble – we would need these, as we would not have a telly. Each box was judiciously marked 'Winter Clothes' or 'Board Games'. I felt smug doing this, using Heather's flatpack secondhand boxes and a large black pen *especially for the job*. The Correct Tools. I overwrote 'Sewing Machine/Blue Throws' with my own version, and felt I was Doing Things Properly. Even then I had some premonition that it might not work out like that.

In order to pack the van more efficiently, James unpacked most of the boxes.

'They were an awkward shape,' he said.

By unpacking the boxes, he managed to condense most of our possessions into odd nooks and crannies in the van. Which was great – a practical use of limited space. Unfortunately however, what this meant was that when everything was *un*packed at the French end, nothing had an immediate box-home to live in. So there was an extreme juxtaposition of items and articles. This would perhaps have been charming and incongruous in a conventional ready-made house context (Look! A CD next to a saucepan!) but in this instance it meant everything was thrown together; a tumbling assemblage in a roofspace brown with decades of dirt, the objects lying on a fluffy brown layer of filth. This made me more miserable than anything, at first.

When we got here, James unpacked the van pretty much single-handedly. It was raining: he was exhausted. He threw everything up into the 'attic' – this roofspace, thick with accumulated dirt, lit by one small glass roof tile. Clothes, boots, books, pans, all landed cheek by jowl, with no fixed place to live. The sight of these everyday items in disarray shocked me. Joe's clothes cupboard stood amid wood, plastic bottles for recycling, concrete dust and rubble, the surface of the cupboard beginning to get covered in birdpoo. It was horrible.

I didn't say much, the first few days. On the third night, I woke in the early hours, my mind crystal-clear with the certainty that I should leave, and take the kids with me, back to Wales. I could rent a house, maybe the house I had just come from, and stop this terrible situation for them and myself. In the night, I visualise the beds we have left behind, rectangular and wide, with the clean sheets I left on them, in the wide, light rooms. Dry and spacious and established. Safe. My mind races through the practicalities – not consciously thinking about things, as such, already knowing what has to be done and why. This ridiculous and impossibly difficult situation could be fixed and I will fix it. I will get the ferry back. We will sell the barn. I am decided.

The conversation. James and I speak and I tell him of my intent. I sit with Joe and Anna at the kitchen table. I think they will be gladdened by this new departure, their misery removed.

I say, 'We will sell the barn and move back to Wales.'

Anna says, in a voice I have never heard before – a quiet, soft voice, 'But what about Dad's dream?'

And Joe says, 'No,' and writes down why he does not want to do that. He says that his dad has been through too much, and that if we left it would make it 'all for nothing.' They amaze me, these children. And it is them – their love, strength and insight, that really holds it together. So we stay. I am stunned and chastened.

Joe finds his spot on the large brown sofa and determinedly sets up his Xbox in the kitchen-cum-living room, directly under the hole where the stairs will go. The tangle of wires snake around and the screen seems incongruous in this setting.

'Where's the paddling pool?' asks Anna. 'Where's the keyboard?'

In the first days *petits filous* neighbouring children, here for a wedding party, run laughingly along the tracks, a gaggle of cousins of all ages, calling to each other. Mosquito-bitten and pale, Joe and Anna emerge from a darkened room where they watch Hollywood DVDs back to back. Who can blame them? Safety in the known. They come out and meet the neighbours, standing under Msr Le Métayer's beautiful oak tree on that perfect lawn.

I have realised that unless you write it immediately, or very near to the time it has happened, the moment and its feeling vanish very quickly. Like childbirth, the pain evaporates, until all that is left are the words that describe. So I can relate sleeping in the tent the first few weeks, but what I can't perhaps communicate now is the empty terror that was in my heart.

The second week of sleeping in the caravan, I had to pitch the large eight-man tent, to get out of such close living. It was hot work. The children watched as I puffed over poles and nylon. James commented on my work. The ground was hard, the tent pegs bent. When I had got it up, I set out the bedrooms. Anna became interested then and it turned into glamping: an inflatable mattress, several billion throws. I was glad we had the glamour angle because personally I felt it was more like refugee-ing, but didn't like to say.

I wanted to sleep in a tent so that I did not have to walk over anyone to get in or out of bed. I wanted to sleep in a tent as the air would be cooler.

In tents, particularly in tents in a rural French outback, one is conscious always of the Axe-Wielding-Maniac. That, and the Rabid Hound. What you notice in tents is that *sounds travel at night*. So don't worry if a cow sounds unnervingly close, or whether that cawing noise is an owl or a vulture, *they can't harm you.* You will, naturally, be perfectly self-assured about that. This is Europe, after all and we do not generally have life-threatening animals. You will feel perfectly assured of this until you sleep in the tent. Then, the tropical squawks and mournful hoots hold you paralysed in good old primaeval fear for hours at a time. You do not look at a watch, so even time itself is formless, like the night. The acorns popping, hot from the tree, resonate through your very soul as you lie waiting, waiting, for the glorious dawn to come. Perhaps you step out in your practical white faux-Crocs to let any would-be fox know that you are There; you are Human, you Will Not Be Fucked With. Brave, unzipping the tent, whoknowswhat lying beyond the wet flaps. You wee near a stone and stuff the loo-roll under it. Sometimes it is very fucking weirdly moony light. Sometimes you hear muted voices and fireworks, and you wonder where the party is and why you are never there. Sometimes you hear a cough, and there is no explanation.

I tell James I got up and out in the night and had a wee next to the tent, 'just so the fox knows I am there.'

'That's very… animal,' he says. I think he is a bit bemused.

Anna thinks nothing of it. I let her sleep the side nearest the trees. The loud tropical squawking is a *green woodpecker!* Duh. Of course. What was I thinking.

I'm writing this because everyone wants to know, everyone wants to see pictures, everyone thinks it is Living The Dream. Everyone sees it with their own vision and I'm not sure anyone wants to be told the reality of it. I think their ears blank off at that point. They want to be shown pictures on Facebook, with continuous blogs and updates of the quaint charm of rustic rural Breton living. Pictures of the barn's progress as it gets done-up. I think of 'Before' and 'After' pictures, of gravelled approaches, wide wooden planters, painted ironwork, the stonework photoshopped into a cohesive whole. It is so easy in pictures, so swift.

We drive the children to meet their cousins, aunties and uncles who are holidaying further south. They will spend a few days with them at the Eurocamp. It is their treat. We don't have car cover, it is a long drive, we are skint and afraid of breaking down on the way. We set off early, in the dark, before the roads get hot. We arrive to a sleeping campsite, the tents pitched cheek-by-jowl, a holiday suburbia by the sea. Sad in the morning drizzle, dead barbecues and the hard-packed earth of many families' bodies.

We drop off the kids and they make for the pool, happy to be in holiday mode, happy to be with people they know, with family. James and I set off on the drive home up through the Vendée, past whitewashed houses with red tile roofs, flat salt plains.

We drive home over the massive bridge at St Nazaire.

'Very Orwelian,' says James. I think he is referring to the 'ZONE EXPÉRIMENTALE' signs, fluorescent hazard barriers to the right of the road, but no. He nods towards a huge industrial ruin, a brown-brick edifice against the plateau of St Nazaire.

'Oh, that.'

In the wake of that building, to our right, in the common no-man's-land between the autoroute and the next service station, lies a field a couple of acres wide. White shimmer in the heat.

'Gypsies,' says James.

It is only then that I notice the caravans, hundreds of them, speading across the poor land. Caravans and white vans, reflecting the sunlight as far as the eye can see. *New* white trucks, *new* caravans. The Gypsies of St Nazaire.

God, but they must be hot. There is no shade, no shelter, no tree.

'Where do they poo and wee?' I ask.

James decides not to answer that one. Some of the caravans have strange netting over them, which doesn't reach the ground. Perhaps it keeps the flies off, we think. It is rough. It is the sort of rough that I hadn't truly noticed before, the sort of circumstantial rough you notice when you are close to that circumstantial roughness yourself. And we've got a white van.

We arrive back at the barn and I spend a couple of hours weaving a fence out of strips of young chestnut. My stomach aches and gripes. We pick up the kids a couple of days later. They arrive back at the barn in understandably bad moods – they already miss their cousins and the holiday spirit.

In the kitchen 'pod' within the barn, we have to make sure the chairs (plastic, picnic-table ones) are pulled away from the table when we leave the room. That way the mouse can't climb up the chairlegs onto the table. The first mouse he catches, James drives 10km from the house and releases into the countryside around Pontivy. The second mouse he finds eating his baguette in full view on the kitchen table. This time he gets Angry. He avoids the Traps and Poison from the extensive selection at Brico Baud and chooses instead an 80-*centime* traditional wooden number. 'Lucifer' it's called, and it has pretty nifty typography and an impressed monochrome illustration of a mouse on it. I scoff that it looks like something out of *The Dandy*, that there is No Way he will catch anything with that. I put money on it. 50 euros. The children exult. The next day he catches the mouse.

Feeling like a refugee. Not having the language. I have a sense of what being a refugee must be like: not just the language, but also the basic essential requirements to keep oneself clean, fed, warm. These things take up a lot of energy, if you don't have easy means. It is a hackneyed thought perhaps, but I think of the monotony and downbeating nature of flies. What is the point of swiping them away if they just come and land back on you? How much more infinitely miserable must it be to live without running water, or electricity.

Survival. James talks about 'not dying' in the early days, and I feel subjugated with misery. I don't want to 'survive', I think. I want to 'Live'. I want hot baths and clean sheets in wide bedrooms. I want meals out, fresh clothes and perfumed hair. I don't want to 'survive' in a barn. How have I come to this? 'This' can be, could be, so much more. The potential still remains. Plus, of course, there are not many other great alternatives that wouldn't upset the family beyond measure.

Neighbours

Things I have learnt about French people so far: they are very interested in food. Very. Coming as I do from a background where not-burning-the-fishfingers is a sign of culinary achievement, this is a revelation. They talk about the ingredients and process of making a meal as a large topic of conversation. Our neighbours are friendly and welcoming, they make us elaborate meals and forgive me my lousy French. They are good people, slightly puzzled at our choosing to live in this place, in this way. I am taught new words at a rapid rate, words you just don't get at regular French class. I come home to the barn after evenings out with the neighbours with words like *velouté* and *le renard* swirling in my head, threads of conversations and phrases.

We go to dinner at Thérèse and Michel's place. They live in part of the turreted house at the bottom of the track, by the pond. They rent it off the *maire* and his wife, who live in the other part. Below the house is a small watermill, with a cottage that is rented out as a *gîte* – people come to fish and boat. The landscaped gardens roll down to the river and a field of llamas, which the *maire*'s wife keeps as a sort of miniature zoo.

We scrub up and shower and arrive fresh for dinner at the time specified. Only on the doorstep do we realise we are too early. Michel shows us around the llamas and I pretend to be fearless as they nibble and nudge me. Anna is not convinced.

We eat outside, a simple-but-elaborate sequence of dishes. We have black grapes in crushed pistachios, cut lengthways as purple ovals. There is honeyed cheese and other things which must have taken all day to prepare. Thérèse is easy-going and relaxed, short and brown with curly hair. In her early 50s, she has no children, though Michel has a son, Kevin, from his previous marriage. We saw Kevin playing the trumpet out on the front lawn once, as we drove past on our way home. They were having a *soirée*, small clutches of people in pastel shirts under the tall trees – you could almost see the *cologne*.

Thérèse has no English, so we spend time with her old school dictionary which she digs out, waving it triumphantly. She invites me to Yoga classes. Michel's English is perfect, and he takes pleasure in it. Although not a drinker himself, he likes to present us with an assortment of selected wines, which match the dishes we are eating. Conversation flows easily. It's a late night, and we walk home in the pitch black, holding on to each other as we find our way onto the track.

The mayor's wife has been round to the barn already, treading through the dark interior, intrigued by what we are up to. She examines the building through the thick lens of her glasses, listening carefully to our plans. 'Oh la-la!' she exclaims, gesticulating at the grand amount of work to be done. She has a contained energy; practical, kind, effusive but not fussy, if that is possible. We see her husband the mayor often, walking slowly around his pond in the green shade. We always stop to say hello, and he always shakes hands warmly. There never seems to be a rush.

The mayor's wife bumps up the track one day, skids to a halt and emerges in a flurry of dust to invite us for traditional *crêpes* at her home. This time we are studiedly late. We scrub up and arrive on the doorstep with cider and wine. We realise we're late – when the mayor's wife says a time, she *means* that time. When Michel says a time, he actually means half an hour to an hour later. Michel and Thérèse are there at the meal, casual and familiar, along with the mayor. We do a lot of kissing; cheek to cheek then cheek to cheek again.

It's a very informal dinner, over the round kitchen-table. Madame rustles up *crêpe* after *crêpe*, in her pinny, surrounded by a halo of light-blue smoke. We have *crêpes* with Nutella, with *citron*, *saucisson* ... they keep on coming. There is a constant simmer of conversation; *Monsieur le Mayor* talks about the mushrooms he will hunt in the autumn. There are other, faster conversations, about relatives and neighbours and hairdressers, that I have no hope of following. I am very shy at these dinners, though I don't think I show it.

Madame takes us into the lounge, a light, formal room beneath the curved turret feature of the house. She shows us black and white photographs of herself as a young woman, in stiff formal Breton outfits.

'Oh la-la!' she exclaims, waving her hands, and Anna and I can't help laughing.

Though they are obviously wealthy people – the place is pristine, there's a big silver Merc outside – there is no standing on ceremony, and it is not ostentatious. We arrive home 'french-fried' with the strain of trying to understand it all, trying to keep up, to make sense and contribute intelligibly.

We go for *áperos* with Sue, Tim and their daughter Molly, a family from Yorkshire who have lived here the past seven years. They are friendly and jocular. Anna and I make eyes at the pool: she plays with their big old dog. Molly is out with her boyfriend.

Sometimes we go to meals and barbecues with James's new friends – Phil, the larger-than-life builder and Françoise, his *petite* French girlfriend. A self-employed translator, she has two young children from previous partners. Françoise and I talk about schooling and work. She mentions that being salaried, rather than self-employed, is the preferred French way. The kids charge around outside with other children – French and English – who are at the meal. There are English folk who have lived here for some time – plasterers, labourers, seasonal rose-pickers. One northern couple moved here because of the climate; she smokes cannabis to ease her chronic arthritis. Some of them have bought additional small houses and are doing them up. One woman, despite having lived here for so long, still misses England and makes up for it with *Eastenders* via satellite and extended family visits. Late into the night we sit in long rows along the table amidst the empty bottles, and I drive us home across the D roads even later.

One day James takes me to meet a woman he has met at one of these gatherings. Rebecca is an older, Australian woman who wants him to come and look at her 'project'. She has a property above St Barthélemy which she is turning into an Art Centre and Retreat. She rings one day when James is out and is pleased to introduce herself and invite us up to lunch. She is interested in what I do – designing, some art work – and thinks there will be plenty of scope for us to talk about all sorts of ideas.

We drive up later in the week, navigating the intricate backroads and points of reference (left at the cowshed) to her house. From outside it looks semi-detached, with a small front-garden. Rebecca opens the door and we walk into a cool, dark interior, furnished with ornate carved wood, richly coloured textiles and lots and lots of paintings. Everything in that house is carefully chosen, considered and placed. She shows us from room to room; it is quite beautiful, simple and elegant. Rebecca is tall, with long dark hair and a deep, calm voice. Lunch is risotto, and cake for dessert. Lots of tea in china cups. Lots of conversation and talk of James's work, then we head out to see the project, following her red Peugeot.

On nearing the project – what looks like a farm on top of the hill – we see a tall figure clad in denim walking towards us. James stops and greets Rebecca's son Raphael, who happens to be blond and blue-eyed. To say he had piercing blue eyes would be a cliché. He has *the most* piercing blue eyes. He is wearing a cowboy hat.

'James! So good to see you' he purrs. 'Jane! so good to meet you!'

He shakes my hand through the car's open window, and we kiss cheek to cheek. He smells gorgeous.

'You smell gorgeous,' I say.

'Chanel,' he gleams.

We explain we are following Rebecca to look at her project.

'Fantastic!'

He tells us he has just been talking to Apple about some forthcoming work and booking a flight to Milan. Now he is walking back to the house for lunch.

We say our goodbyes and continue on our way. This must be the son James told me he met at Phil's party, along with his Italian boyfriend.

We pull up outside the main building, long stone barns on either side of it. Rebecca leads the way into the house, through two metal sliding doors, just like ours. The first room we stand in is obviously the old dining room – it is stone, unplastered, but one wall is completely taken up with an enormous painting – several figures, Breton women, in a primitive, colourful style. There is a large table, with formal dining chairs, as though set out for a medieval feast. Rebecca takes us in, then out and around a complex of buildings, all of which are in a state of major disrepair and dereliction, all the while talking us through her visualisation.

'These will be the open studios,' she says, waving a hand at the old cow sheds, grey concrete and gridwork. The way she describes them, I can see it: an artistic mirage under the hot sun, some middle-aged American potter crouched over his wheel, a young muse sitting nearby, reading Salinger while the hangings billow softly in the gentle breeze.

'We'll work in metal, clay. I like working with metal.'

She leads us on to the upper part of the building. The stairs are unsafe and this is what she wants to talk to James about. There are several large rooms which have been knocked together, ceramic rubble from a dismantled bathroom, holes in the floor.

'This will be apartments,' she says.

I have to believe her, I guess, though even I am struggling to see it, by this point. It's so *big*. And she is talking about it being open to paying guests in the *very near future*.

We walk around the back, through recently mown undergrowth and a lot of nettles. There is a guy back there, stroking a chicken. He welcomes us with an open smile and carries on stroking his chicken. Rich is Rebecca's other son. He is broader, earthier, generally more heterosexual than his brother. He lives here most of the time, doing most of the work, making a vegetable garden and writing a screenplay.

He bought the hens for two euros apiece in the market, and they live in a box in the kitchen for now. They're a bit hesitant but he's encouraging them to come out of their box and wander around a bit. I like him immediately and we talk at great length, while Rebecca and James look at the proposed carpentry work. Rich and I stand in the kitchen garden, I talk nineteen to the dozen and laugh a lot, which I haven't done for a while. He talks about the angry farmer next door, cleaning toilets in town for a bit of cash, and the Mayan calendar. Rich is preparing for the end of the world, from what I can make out. He has great, even teeth and grew up in Tahiti. There is something essentially calming about all this. I have no idea why, but I like these people, even though they are obviously mad, and possibly charlatans.

There are some people, like my friend Sophie and my cousin Joel, who have an astonishing knack of making derelict buildings *chic*. They seem to rise to the occasion, to instinctively know what these grandiose wrecks need – that is, larger than life, stage-set furnishings. They nonchalantly style them, and nobody gives a fuck whether the toilet works or not, because there is a jam jar of giant blooms on the side, *Interiors* magazine and *Shells of the Shore* to look at.

Somehow, the dirt and squalor become elevated to art status, so that you notice the *verdigris* patina within a knackered windowledge, but it doesn't gnaw at you in its miserableness. It doesn't matter if the bed (it has to be a huge, huge, bed) is visible from the bog, or the kitchen. It's very clever – I don't think it's haphazard – they know how to use the right colour to pick out a spot; they select just the right object, to make it all work, somehow.

Rebecca used to lecture in Interior Design, she tells me.

'A lot of the girls were young mothers. They were poor and couldn't afford the things in shops. I used to tell them that everything they needed, they would find to hand.'

Much of Rebecca's furniture has been imported from Australia, Tahiti and Spain. She takes us into another massive stone barn where there are boxes and crates of her belongings, still unpacked. The birds are pooing on them, which she's a bit pissed off about. Some of the furniture she has sourced from a *bricolage* in Vannes over the past twenty years. It sounds like the authentic, bargain basement *bricolage* which I yearn for. She says she'll take me there one day. In the meantime, do we want any chairs?

On leaving the place, slightly dazed at the scale of their ideas, James and I are quiet. Our ambitions seem so much more modest in comparison, and that suits me fine. Back at the barn, James points out a toad, which is sitting very still just outside the kitchen door. James is quietly delighted. I am quietly ambivalent. I am sure toads are very unusual creatures. I'm sure they are spiritually benevolent and biologically fascinating. They don't move much, and will make like leaves when they're disturbed in undergrowth. I'd prefer it if they didn't come inside.

I think about space, about scale, about privacy and the idea of 'retreat'. Although the barn seems remote, some days the world and his brother pass by. Early in the morning the pigfarmer zips down in his little white van, does something to the pigs (probably checks a thermostat) and zips back off again. Msr Le Métayer – Ange – arrives in his old silver Renault to tend his vegetable garden. We might see Thérèse power-walking up the track – she has quit smoking and is concerned about putting on weight. Sometimes Michel is with her, kitted out in jogging gear.

'Salut Michel! Salut Thérèse!'

Then there are the ramblers. Here they come: a compact murmuring crowd of correctly-attired walkers, who gaze curiously at our set-up as they gaggle up the track, with boots and sticks and field glasses. There is nothing to shield us from view, apart from the camelia and the small fir tree, which have grown perhaps six inches in five years. When the dutch barn was originally set in the land, all the top soil must have been taken away to level the ground. Now the barn is gone it creates a flat lawn, but the earth is poor and dry.

I think of the informal hedge I want to plant, to create a screen, a barrier between our patch and the track. So that we are not looked at straight-on, by all who pass by.

'Be bold,' Rebecca says.

She has 'dressed' her house; it is opulent and ornate inside. The garden is private. If I created a private space, it might help to cushion me against what I feel are the extremities of life, of this living.

A weekday before the kids start school, it is overcast, hot and oppressive. I take myself off for a bike ride after lunch and cycle up the track to the small roads that criss-cross the landscape. In Wales the mountains dominate the skyline, here the vistas are more open. The corn is tall against the telegraph poles lining the lonely road, Pluméliau church spire in the distance. I come to what looks like a bus shelter, faded brown clapboard at the T-junction. Loosely gathered around it are a few kids – young teenage boys and girls, kicking about in the dust. One lad sits on his own some way off, crosslegged on the tarmac, with a big golden mutt. He doesn't look up as I cycle past.

The gang watch me with keen interest as I approach. I might look a bit unkempt, I realise. I'm wearing a stripey turban, T-shirt, old grey skirt and dodgy Crocs. We exchange *Bonjours* and I check them out as I cycle past; the dark-haired girls, a couple of lads, one with spiky hair who is obviously the ringleader. He mentions the word *velo* and makes his mates snicker as I cycle past. I think I might be the most interesting thing that has happened round these parts for a while. It's reassuring, that bored teenagers, bus shelters and dog-end days of summer are the same wherever you are.

I also think: Young Teens = Possible Friend Material for Joe and Anna. The spiky-haired lad's comments have made me flush with embarrassment, of course – I imagine (i.e. know) that I look like some middle-aged hippy on a clapped-out cycle. But experience tells me that they might be more shy of me, than I am of them. Also, of course, I am older, which must mean I have some authority, right?

I think of all these things as I cycle onwards towards Pluméliau, the road gently curving and flat. I think to myself that my mum would probably have made friends with the local children by now, that they would all be back at our gaff, making themselves at home, generally hanging out. Actually, if it was my mum, they'd probably be in their very own pantomime by now. I reason to myself that I am going to talk to these children on the way back. I'm going to introduce myself, let them know who and where we are, so that if they are ever passing, they can drop by. I also know that if Joe and Anna had any whiff that I was doing this, they would be mortified.

So I turn back and they're still there, bored stiff at the T-junction. I come to a slow halt and dismount. They gather round and I bravely do my introduction and they all introduce themselves – Aurélie, Océane, Vincent and Kevin, the one with the spiky hair. They are shy and smiling, telling me which schools they go to, where the buses pick up and drop off. I cycle off with waves all round and the stasis of the day is broken.

One afternoon a large old car comes bumping down the track – sunshine bouncing off silver, dust hanging behind. It comes slowly to a halt. We stand in the heat watching as Monsieur Le Métayer helps out his wife, Madame Le Métayer. She is a tiny woman, with starling bones. She wears a sateen yellow blouse with a bow at the neck; her hair is dark and her skin is pale. Madame is very frail and we slowly show them into our kitchen and offer them drinks. She meets the children and exclaims at it all, fascinated by what we have done and are doing.

We spend some time outside, looking at the land and discussing the soil. We walk around to the front of the barn as she tells us how they used to live in this building, when their children were babies, before they built the white villa next door. She points to where there used to be a spring, under what is now the gravelled track. She shakes her head and says *dur* a lot. *Dur* means hard. I can't make out whether she is referring to her past, or our present. Perhaps both.

We walk over to Monsieur Le Métayer's veg patch – immaculate rows of leeks stock-still in the late summer sunshine. Grapes cluster along the vines. Madame is keen to inform us the pigshed will shut down next year. She is emphatic and it seems she is the boss. We go home laden with *haricots verts* and pumpkins.

Institutional Chartreuse

Kafka-esque: James's description of the strange militancy of French organisation, of time stood still, or somehow warped in *patisserie* doorways.

The school is large and determinedly modern, with unnecessarily-angled windows along the sides. The newly planted trees are struggling to maintain a grasp in the parched earth on the covered approaches. Michel takes us in the back way; he is a teacher and our neighbour. Although this school is the closest to us geographically, it is not in our administrative area. We couldn't have got them into this school without help.

The walls are an extraordinary green: *institutional chartreuse*. There are no pictures or adornment on the walls. There are plants, however, arranged in pots of three – pretty Zen. The stairwells are surrounded by glass; it is large and light. The seats outside the Principal's office are red, as is the whole front of the building. We shuffle into her office after she gets back from lunch. The Principal wears a cream trouser suit and is quite comfortable in her position of authority, listening to Michel's explanation of who we are and why we're here. He seems to be assuring her we are not simply English dilettantes; he talks on and on. It is only when James adds to this, in fluent French, that she begins to take notice. She takes our paperwork – reports from the kids' previous Welsh schools, Joe's secondary school crest looking important, Anna's bilingual primary report. Joe has two years of French from his secondary school, Anna has much less, just the private lessons we managed before we came out.

It is settled then, very quickly, with a sweep of the hand. She will accept both children into the school: Anna will go into *sixième* and Joe into *quatrième*. There is no linguistic support, but she will try to arrange something. There are only three other English children in the school, who have been here throughout the system and are all fluent.

The wheels are put in motion. There is a mass of paperwork, an awesome number of forms that seem to arrive on a daily basis in the few weeks before school starts. Social Security numbers, Doctor's contact details, school dinner information. James locates where to apply for bus passes and I take the children to get photos for their ID cards – we spend a long time swizzling the photo-booth chair up and down. Then on to get many immunisations. On Saturday morning we drive to the *collège* to collect a box apiece containing all the kit they will need for their particular year. Everybody gathers within the wide reception area – we meet Molly and Sue as we line up for our boxes. Molly is enrolling at this school to re-take ('double') her last year. Although she passed her general certificate, she needs to improve her grades, before she goes on to *lycèe*.

Back at home Anna unpacks her cardboard box and tries out all the contents. There are protractors, set-squares, compass, paints and brushes, rulers, a variety of pens (including highlighters), file dividers, plastic wallets, hole-punch guards. There are many exercise books, with different sorts of paper. Anna spends a long time inspecting this paraphernalia and prepping up her school bag. Joe's box lies untouched where it landed.

The first day Anna starts school, we gather in the playground as the children are called to their groups. All the children look the same. There is a certain reassuring quality to this – seeing the same sort of long hair, the same sort of hooded jumper, cardigan and backpack, carefully chosen and worn. Too high up on the back, and you'd get bullied, apparently. Bags have to be worn low.

It is cold and the concrete is grey; the wind whips along the hard edges of the building. The principal is smart in suit and scarf, standing on top of the steps. I catch the bit in her talk about bubblegum being prohibited and don't understand a word of the rest. Other French families watch their children as their names are called to their form groups. Anna's name is called somewhere in the middle and James and I watch her walk away with her group.

What chance has she got? I think.

In the car, on the way back, I cannot speak. I am struck dumb. I wear big sunglasses and make no sound as the tears fall down my cheeks unimpeded. I am being quiet because Joe is in the back – his first day at school is tomorrow. The pain and fury I feel towards James at this point is unspeakable. I think it is only the liquid venom – like petrol – of my anger, that sustains me. Unmitigated liquid fury.

How could he put us in this position? I think. Why take us from one set of institutional structures to another? What was wrong with the first one? Why, when I know all the ins-and-outs of the British educational system, put me in a situation where I cannot support my children at all? I am programmed to organise, to educate, to communicate. In this context I can do none of those things. And I think that it will never be okay.

Later, in the playground, the very same day, when we return to pick her up, I see her through the plate glass window. She is outside in the yard, amidst all the other children, in a huddle with her friends. She looks up to wave. It is astonishing. She shows us the work she has been doing in English – finding the phrases she thinks 'might be useful,' should she need them.

Joe starts the next day. Two very lively girls seem to gravitate towards him straight away. He is cool; he is calm. The first day, he makes a whole host of new friends, they play 'babyfoot' in the breaktimes and long lunch period. Anna explains the process of lunch-time, and demonstrates how she holds her hand under the electronic scanner. The children in turn now have their own enormous set of paperwork – journals, timetables, diaries. They navigate the complex arrangements of lockers and room allocations.

Some days the kids are so exhausted they literally can't speak, dealing as they are with the massive complexities of a new language, new culture and new school. I have the utmost respect for them: they are way out of my league. I try to make things pleasant for them in the small ways I can, though sometimes this feels infinitesimally small.

The first few weeks we conjugate a lot of verbs. Joe goes on several outdoor trips – orienteering and to play volleyball on the beach. There is a cycling event organised on a Wednesday afternoon which he takes part in. At the time, I don't think too much about it. It is only later, when I return to pick them up and see them whizzing back into the school yard, fearsomely fast, narrow tyres on hard concrete, that my heart is in my mouth. I realise this is serious stuff.

The school has a fleet of mountain bikes which they transport into the woods. Joe regales me with talk of tears and terrifying inclines at great speed – he didn't cry, but plenty of boys did, he tells me.

'They have all the kit, lycra leggings and water bottles and that. But if a chain comes off they don't know what to do.'

Joe can do chains; in fact, he seems to be able to do all of it, thriving on this outdoor exercise.

Anna runs cross-country. On the coldest morning the whole school is turfed out into the local stadium. One girl 'fainted with cold' and had to be carried off the track, wrapped in a duvet. Anna is stoical. It all sounds rather shocking, to me. They have a 'Breakfast Club' – she is horrified at the meagre bread-and-water 'traditional' French experiences of her contemporaries. She is very wary of school food, eating only very little of the three-course lunches.

It is worth remembering that seminal books such as *On Walden Pond* were not written with a wife and two children in tow. It is probably easier to extol the virtues of the great outdoors and Nature when you don't have to drop the kids off at school and get the shopping in. And old Paul Brunton can be meditating like mad, but again, it is tricky to be spiritual when there's homework on the table. Same can be said for *Pilgrim at Tinker Creek*, and all that lot. Nowhere, as I recall, does she mention doing the laundry. If she did, it would involve the Creek, most probably. And some stones. Could take the whole day, no doubt, with the faint essence of woodsmoke in the drying process. *Oh! C'est charmant!* But we are in the 21st century here, with the requirements of a 100% synthetic sports kit for Joe, and the alienation of small town shopping malls. There seems to be no way out of this, and some sadistic part of me is gleeful that James has to endure the same nylon trauma of The Sports Shop, as I have done, which must be the same branded hell the world over.

We begin to settle into a tentative routine. In the mornings, I drop them off in Pluméliau, and they get the big continental bus the rest of the way into Baud. I am home in ten minutes, have breakfast, clear up and do some work before going for a walk up the track. Now in the pod kitchen there are light fittings, but they are not necessarily attached to anything.

I go to the UK on a three-day work trip. Plane journey. I sit next to a sprightly widow of 80, who tells me of her daughter's relocation to France seven years ago. A success story, the daughter determined to learn the language, which she did within six months. The children were aged 15 and 11 when they moved over. Why is it that these people are always called Sharon and Steve and have several properties? They have houses, pools and a BMW that shows you how much space you have when you reverse. On money she says, 'when you don't have it, you know about it.' We talk about UK immigration – she is 'not a racist' but resents all those people moving in, getting houses, healthcare.

Her daughter and husband and family and dog (golden Labrador) are all very happy and healthy and help out English newcomers to France.

She pats me on the arm as we say goodbye.

'You've only been there a short while. Give yourself another year, you'll look much better.'

It's only afterwards I wonder if I really look that bad.

Southampton airport is a blast of people, chocolate bars and crisps. More volume, generally. France suddenly seems a lot simpler, civilised. There are no Mars Bars at eye level, perhaps that's what it is. I travel on to Manchester, then on to Wales and stay at my mum's house for two nights. It it unusual to have a bath and put in hair mousse. When I wash my knees actual *dirt* comes off, which makes me wonder what the shower has been doing all these weeks. I resolve to set-to on the kids.

I go to a large private view, with everybody there. I look good; you know, chunky heels and tight jeans, a loose gold top. Just the right combination of 'thrown together' *chic*. There are a few slight double-takes when I walk in, and a lot of questions. It is strange, being with all these people after being in such intense and different circumstances for so long. Strange and familiar at the same time.

What strikes me is the impression of so many chickens pecking for so much corn. There must be three hundred people at the event, all wanting to be, or being, Artists. Beneath the studied nonchalance, there lies *competition*, cloaked in irony. And that is why I am there too, of course. To do the same, in a way. *Here I am, look at me! I have moved to barn-dwelling and I am Successful! Look – Thinner! Leaner! French-er.*

I don't feel these things at the time, but only afterwards realise how my reference point has changed, my circumstances have changed, that what I am doing has a novelty factor for most people.

I walk towards someone I am obliged to say hello to. She

stands very tall against a wall with her friend and they watch me appraisingly as I walk across the parquet floor, struggling to look relaxed in my too-high heels. We kiss briefly, cheek to cheek.

'You're back *already*!' she says, with a wide, disingenuous smile.

I feel sometimes that when some people ask after me, beneath their sugar-coated questions are other voices, which are not so light and bright and ironic, but which are trying to ascertain what I am really about. I think some people have already established in their own minds that I am deluded. They treat me with a gentle tolerance, given my obvious romanticism in this crazy venture. I can sense some people have a vague distrust of me. Beneath those simple few words then, the subtext I hear is:

Have you failed yet? Have you realised the patent stupidity and naïvety of your ideas and have you returned to lick your wounds and find solace in the Known? If so, I am here as a reference point, someone who Knew, who could have told you from the start. Silly you, thinking that you could change it for the better.

Or maybe I'm imagining things.

That night I lie in my mum's spare room and think intently of my family, lying in the caravan. I close my eyes and take myself over every inch of it, feeling my way along the narrow alleyway between Joe's bed and the broken stove. I know it as exactly the opposite of the art gallery scene – no hype, no glamour, no showing-off. A course in survival, in fact.

I go to the meeting; I write the document. When I get back to the barn, I use the English papers to line the new stairs, and paint the stairwell white. It is a quiet, misty Monday, the Sunday broadsheets ablaze – *6 Weeks to Save the Euro.* It is curiously satisfying treading on Cameron's head as I pad up and down stairs in my bare feet.

When I left my well-paid, full-time job and moved to Brittany, one friend emailed me: *And with one leap, she was free.*

But it wasn't one leap, Dom. It took five years of struggling and wrangling, learning and extricating. It took me that time to realise that I was more miserable managing on my own, in Britain, than I would be living in more difficult circumstances in France. I had all the trappings – rented house, car loan, full-time job, credit card bills, overdraft, all of which were large.

I received a 'Financial Profile' a couple of weeks ago, an A4 document from the bank with a *black* cover with my name in white. This obviously means I am important, right? Why else would they use so much ink? I am obviously a Valued Customer. It showed my year's incomings and outgoings. The amount coming in was a little over £200 *more* than the amount going out. That's all there was in it. So a standstill, if ever there was one. Treading water. Going, financially, nowhere. The whole idea about moving to France was that financially we would be better off. Or at least, that we would start at ground zero, and work out exactly what was necessary and what was not – whether we could make money, rather than living in some overdraft interest-zone.

You can see from the above part of what my relationship with money is. Over the years I've worked and earned, I've had access to borrowed cash, in the form of bank loans and overdrafts, but I've never had the sort of money that provides a major cushion. Money is tied up with property, and my family background is so disjointed that for a long time there was no parental 'home' as such. My nan's flat was my home in my late teens – somewhere I could always return to and always did. My mum and dad divorced when I was very young.

My mum's second husband Ian and I could not get on, so I left that house when I was 16. It suited my dramatic nature, I guess, to leave on my sixteenth birthday, the day I was legally entitled to. I had moved away several times before, because things had often been fractious at home. I went to four secondary schools in as many years. I'm digressing wildly, but I've realised that not only has my background had an impact on what I've done in life, but is also connected to my relationship with money.

I've had an overdraft facility since I was sixteen. I've used it ever since, constantly in the red and only occasionally making inroads onto the right side of the line. So the money I have spent has never been 'real' money – it has always been the bank's. But I always pay money in, and always pull money out – I imagine pretty much like most people; a balancing act leaning slightly to the left. When I was frustrated at living in our mid-terrace and trying to compensate myself and the kids for not having a big garden, I bought things on credit card – a laptop, a TV. I spent money I didn't have then and don't have now. Most people do, there's nothing unusual in that. But some people show great restraint, and *do not buy what they can't afford.*

What an interesting sentence: do not buy what they can't afford.

I think I have always wanted to be perceived as an independent person who managed very well, so it gave me a sense of pride and security to know I could pay for a ferry crossing, an extra-large bill, a website, a cement mixer, a bank loan, a septic tank, a pair of shoes… Also, because I am generous, I like to give things. *But what about when you can't AFFORD to give things?*

It's an interesting avenue for me, because if I hadn't jumped about with bank loans for so long, I wouldn't have done a postgraduate course, or bought the computer to set up as a designer, or secured a mortgage. My life would have been less fluid, perhaps; it would not have moved ahead in the way it has.

Anyway. Money. We haven't got any. We haven't not-got any either, though, now we do not have a mortgage. We still have debt to pay, but it is decreasing, in smaller sums and there is an end – perhaps two years – in sight.

If you have a mortgage of £125,000 and you have twenty years to pay it, doesn't the whole thing become a bit abstract? I mean, if you *know* you can't afford to pay it off, why bother trying any more? I have friends who periodically put another £10K on their mortgage, to get them over a hump, to wipe a slate clean, that sort of thing. I've done it consistently myself. The repayments add up to an affordable sum every month, so why not? At some point they will probably inherit, or sell their house and buy a cheaper one.

This idea of borrowing on the equity of your house was how we managed to buy the barn in the first place.

Now I sit here in the *collège* parking lot waiting for the children to come out of school. I arrive early and people-watch. The back of other women's cars: bigger, shinier, spick-and-span boots containing woven shopping carriers, denoting Security and Order. The children belonging to these families place their rucksacks in the boot. They are lithe, obliging and unbidden – you just *know* they won't be scattering crumbs of *pain au chocolat* all over the seats on the drive home. Dinner will have been prepared in advance, I imagine – a balanced meal, perhaps a yogurt for dessert. The car seat that provides my vantage point is deeply embedded with ancient chocolate. Abandoned semi-but-not-quite-finished drinks bottles strew the floor, with the customary wrappers and crushed packaging. I wonder if this makes me trailer trash.

Brambles

I make pumpkin soup. It tastes like orange water.

I cut back the brambles along the length of the barn. Scrubby elder and small oaks; the oaks not so small that they transplant easily. In the end I simply cut them down, along with ash and a large holly, which grows straight and strong. I have cut this holly down before, like all the weeds, but they persist, year on year. That forms one of the main reasons for being somewhere full-time, I think – once you have weeded some damn thing, you need to stay on top of it, to keep it at bay.

I pull ivy from the stone walls of the barn. Some comes off in gratifying lengths, some you have to pull and pick at, fingers rough against the stone. Inbetween the stones the wall is packed with dry earth. I worry at one point that the whole thing might come down as I pull a particularly tough piece of ivy – a stone comes with it, the pale red ochre earth crumbling away.

I walk across the garden, from bonfire to barn, my mind wandering from the grey stillness of the day. I begin to warm up with the work. In fact, it's almost tropical.

I realise I want tits like small apples, nipples like acorns; hard, brown, smooth and round. I also want to live in a mortage-free, £200,000 house and have a steady, wealthy and reliable income. I realise this is probably not going to happen working for a provincial Further Education college. I realise that maybe knowing your dream is one step further to achieving it. I want to be thin, brown, relaxed and able to jump James in my bikini top. I fantasise about watching TV in a cool lounge on a hot day, with said bikini top, perhaps an olive spaghetti-strap; either way, the material will be kinda loose in places, y'know? Taking on the concave-chest gang. This is, very evidently, a fantasy.

In the meantime, I am rigorously stripping out extra-long lengths of bramble from the rooftiles, which wind themselves to my socks and tracksuit bottoms. They have me falling over myself, going round in circles like a dog chasing its tail, before I realise they are stuck to me. I curse them. I am wearing the leopard-print socks Mel gave me, with Joe's trainers. *The best fantasies are those that contain some element of truth; that they may actually happen.* The best fantasies.

Life has relaxed a bit now, twelve weeks on, but it's necessary still to hold myself in and up, a lot of the time. Most of the time. Writing here is almost unallowed – it is a luxury of time, of my sitting still while all around me are Things To Do. It is still precarious. It is not perhaps as fragile, though every time I go to pick up the kids from the school bus, I prepare myself for what could be; the tears, the trauma, the end of tether. When we are out of the caravan, it will feel less fragile, I think. You get used to difficult conditions, but they wear you down over time. What may have seemed shocking and squalid becomes familiar – you can still view it as rough, but the impact of it is less acute.

My mum and Charles are coming over at Christmas, so there is a flurry of organisational emails regarding the best dates to stay at Bea's. Bea is my sister (same mum, different dad) who has bought a house a couple of hours south-east of here. I find myself copied into and caught up in the minutiae of these proposed arrangements, whilst simultaneously setting up a new website for James and creating a new account. I get irritated at the details of these emails, think it a diversion from what remains my main quest for some time to come: i.e. to build, and support the building of, a house.

We go to Anna's Parents' Evening. My spirits dim as my lack of language is evident, and brighten again at the fact that I understand most of what the FLE (*Français Langue Étrangère*), or French As a Foreign Language, teacher tells us.

'She is doing good, but it is best to give her ease in places.'

The children's timetable is so intense, with a nine-hour day of undiluted French, that 'ease' is what we will try to give her at home.

Her teachers are good women; respectful, kind, and they genuinely like Anna. The FLE teacher, Madame le Guillenff, is on loan to the school – she is really a German supply teacher, so we don't know how long she'll be here. We very much hope that it will be for six months or more, but she may get moved on next week. She's so important for both Joe and Anna. She is very Breton looking – a bit like me; dark hair, big boned, strong face. I determine to learn the language. Too long I have been lying stagnant.

Back at the barn bedroom Number 1 is on its way. Anna is quietly delighted that it is going 'so quickly' – James laying up wood and drilling constantly the last few days. Anna has already established what will go where – the arrangement of all her objects – stereo, bed, lamp, cupboards… I'd forgotten we had all that stuff and can visualise it as she explains the plan to me in the bare boxed-wood room.

Everything James makes is absorbed into our living as quickly, or quicker, than he makes it. So, the stairs, the bathroom, are swiftly appropriated. It is delicious to leave clothes in a heap on the bathroom floor, a sign of civilisation. The bathroom is tiny, just large enough to house the corner bath James salvaged from a job. I scrubbed it and he double-scrubbed it and it is fine. The bathroom is above the kitchen so the chimney flue runs through the room, making it warm and toasty and drying all the towels. We have painted the floor violet and the walls white, hung up the black oval mirror. As fast as he is working, we are behind him, ready to move in to the space he has created. He works constantly, making stairs for clients too.

I try to untangle my mind today in a five-minute walk up the track after dinner. It's grey, still, but not cold. I realise that not only do we have a language to learn, a house to build, but that this is:

A New Country.

A New Language.

A New House.

A New Business (make that two).

So it is inevitable that it is a bit of a Challenge.

And it won't all happen at once; small steps, every day. Energy can't get diverted into dates and times of meetings with family, because energy is taken up with remaining in stable form while sleeping in a caravan. Joe is still on that foam mattress on the floor. It is not damp. I do feel the damp on my patch of bed, so I sleep in fleece pyjamas in between two duvets. I haven't slept that well the last couple of nights. The moon is bright. The damp seemed worse in sunny weather though; I think the heat pulled it up through the mattress. I feel a little clammy and spotty and could do with a week in a Spa Retreat. I fantasise a little about flat daybeds and warm stones on my stiff back.

I know all these things are a diversion, and that we have to keep on keeping on – learning a little language every day, not making it a chore, maintaining my patience as the irritability of living in such close proximity remains. Buying and preparing edible food (avoiding outlandish online Delia recipes) and working when I can – when the day is clear.

I see the only true way forward as continued application: building bedrooms one by one. Furnishing them, then going with James somewhere, when we take a natural break.

We go to a large Brico depot in Lorient, and James spends a long time looking at fixings for window shutters for other people's houses. Case of the cobbler's children. We look at paint. We buy some sable water-based paint for the strip of landing floor. While he is looking at bolts for a *long* time, I wander over to the lighting section. I pick up a cheap track of spotlights. These lights will enable us to see properly in all parts of the kitchen. Where we now have a naked yellowish bulb, with these there will be spotlight and brightness. It will mean we can see the handwritten notes on Anna's homework.

I take the lighting back to show James. His aisle has filled up with an assortment of the bolt-buying community – predominantly male, they have a particular fashion code and are slightly stooped, poring over small pieces of metal. James points out we don't yet have a proper ceiling. I concede the lights. The bedroom remains number one priority.

Joe is off school with a headache. I am painting the bog. The loo is a small windowless box. All four rooms here are made of combination plywood, the cheapest available. The shower room contains the shower, the loo contains the loo. They are just big enough for the things they hold. The loo is now a white box. Nearly white; it needs another coat over the French emulsion. The smell of thin, fresh paint reminds me of every other house we have ever painted, from a child in a Llanrwst terrace to a bedsit in Bangor, every wall plastered with this covering of new hope, new beginnings. Memories of empty rooms, newspaper and brush-hairs over cobwebs.

Beginnings. I think of that as an FB post, as I transplant the small oaks (which now look as though they are dying). There is a vague triangular arrangement of wheelbarrow, plants, spade, with the lane receding into the sky. A watery sun on early autumn morning. The beginnings of something.

The sable floor paint – French paint pots are *different*; a metal rim like a pie crust that you have to unhook. The paint looks pale brown when I finally get the pot open and swirl it around with a stick. It looks fawn, the dreary sort of colour that certain women wear in layered linen. But on the floor – why, it is delicious, delightful and delovely. It is the sort of pale greenish-grey I have tried to match many times in my dodgy sea-paintings – the colour of northern sea on an overcast November aftenoon – no, wait, it is the colour of earth; mild brown earth. It is, I think, *totally sophisticated*, and much more successful than the pebble colour that I dyed all the towels. I thought pebble would match the champagne bath, you see, but in fact it just looked a dirty, curdled milk colour. I should have done the towels MAGENTA.

But sable, ahhh, sable: yes. It absolutely works. It is not quite sand, it is slightly darker than that, and the very fact it is so indefinable means it is a Success. It is only a stretch of painted wood-floor landing about 6ft x 2, but it transports me to easy living, hot days and cool continental colours.

The barn is visual evidence of how poor we are, which is why it is raw. Also, interestingly, why it is not raw. Because it is so truly evident, there is a clarity to it, for myself and others. There is no choice for me but to enjoy it as much as I can. The reality of the precariousness of money, and a family's health, is my day to day experience.

My hair feels like string and I'm worried about money. I am going grey, a 'distinguished' panel around my temple. The weather has turned chill. There is a strong draught of pigshit as I slide the heavy barn doors closed. They are stiff, unyielding. This procedure reminds me exactly of what sort of circumstances I am in – just in case I get carried away with the cheery and successful posts I've put on Facebook this morning: *James's new site – staircase anybody*? and a piece on TYPO London, the International Design Conference. I think I am very clever. I only hope they pay me, and soon.

There will be a point, I think, where heightened factors of cold, dark and pigshit will combine to form one feeling of overarching depression. It will probably be when I am walking from the caravan to the barn to use the loo. It will probably be at night when I will think, *Ah, so this is how bad it gets*.

So far, there has always been a Mitigating Circumstance – it's been sunny, for example, so that the smell doesn't pervade my consciousness. It used to be that I was like bladderwrack, absorbing the nuances of the weather and my mood changing accordingly. Now I am hardened, and don't let a little rain get me down. Except, of course, it makes everything *wetter*, and more difficult. Anna's bike lies discarded, forlorn. I tell myself it is a sign of activity, of life, but also a sign of unkempt abandonment. I'll bring it in, I'll dry it. It will not rust.

I get wood from the pile in the middle room; more metal sliding doors. Two birds are trapped inside, trying to get out through the old window.

We went to Joe's Parents' Evening. Before setting off we sat in the sun briefly, for me to orient myself to receive the barrage of language. I'd spent the day at the computer, printing documents and reading through them.

We met the French teacher and Maths teacher in the wide reception, to arrange the meetings. There was a fleeting moment where we all stood in the swim – a glimpse of Anna kissing her friend cheek to cheek, Joe in conversation with Madame le Guellanff.

Joe's school report: Maths – *Très bien*. Monsieur Mahé is the maths teacher; he is also Michel, our neighbour. After our *saluts* he takes us swiftly to room 101. Joe is working to a good level, he informs us – contributing and answering questions in class.

'He is a fish in water,' Michel says. 'He is flying!' He swoops his hand.

In French the first thing Madame Le Guellanff said to us was: 'Oh, thank you for Joe!'

She couldn't speak highly enough of him; her eyes twinkled and she smiled. He is *Formidable*.

Formidable! I didn't think they actually *said* that! But they do, and she did. He's: 'Intelligent, articulate, attentive, interested …' Blimey. Is this the same child who demands hot chocolate and fried egg butties on a regular basis, who spends all weekend in his PJs, wrapped in a blue fur jacket, complaining of the cold while the sun shines brilliantly outside? Yes. It is. Madame wants him to complete a FLE Diploma in L'Orient in mid November. She is sure he will pass it, if he works hard. She thinks he'll enjoy the challenge, even though he'll pretend he doesn't. She has a good handle on him. She said she enjoyed working with both Joe and Anna. Joe sings, apparently, when he has finished his work.

'Ils sont gentils,' she says, shaking our hands.

We leave the school in the sunshine, slightly stunned. Joe is speaking French in all the classes, keeping up with *Histoire* and *Géographe*. In the car on the drive home, Anna sings a song she has learnt in *Musique*. It is very French. That evening in the caravan I reflect on their bizarre home conditions and find it hugely relieving that they are managing to survive, and flourish.

Fantastic sun follows misty mornings and cold nights. I pulled out all the oaks I transplanted, as they were quietly dying, and bought some new *cheap* rhododendrons which are now strategically placed on my developing *barrière*. Bamboo is my next mission – I want to try to get to Bignan as there is a *Pépinière* (Nursery) there and also a sculpture park, which I'm going to write an article on. These articles are useful to me, as the dosh comes through on a regular monthly basis.

James has nearly finished Bedroom 1, in between finishing another job. Bedroom 1 is in the eaves and measures about 10ft x 8ft. Chances are we'll all be sleeping in it, to start off with.

Driving to and from the school and shops, we listen to French radio – a bittersweet mix of dodgy 1980s tracks with new French acoustic/pop, all with a slightly melancholic air. Preponderance of Phil Collins, Sting's '*Englishman in New York,*' and '*Bette* bloody *Davis Eyes*' – how did they all get here? Radio Caroline is a graveyard for music that was crap 30 years ago. Then you get these little gems, acoustic harmonies from *Cocoon*.

Yesterday evening I left Anna painting the bedroom while I went to pick up Joe. The bus was late, so I had a moment's lurching stomach that he wasn't on it. He arrived and we went to get a drink from the *8 á* ***Huit***. When we pulled out, we saw Dad passing in his big white van. We were some way behind him, but when we pulled up here at the barn he had just arrived. There was the flurry of Ange leaving. He comes here every day to tend his vegetable garden. They rent out their white villa now and have moved into town, for his wife to be nearer the Doctor's, but he misses this place and can't settle. Ange parks his car in our front yard while he tends his vegetable garden. On my way in and his way out, I flash my lights, he beeps his horn – all very convivial at the end of a working day.

James is working on clients' jobs most of the time and working on the barn the rest. We have to work hard for other people in order to get money, for living costs and building work. The time spent working for clients is time taken away from working on the barn. It is a seemingly impossible Catch-22, which we have discussed many times. Personally, I think it is only possible to build this barn with a big loan, to enable James to work on it full-time. This won't happen because he doesn't want to borrow money, and I can understand that. Therefore we have to do it bit by bit, which will take ages and be a different sort of stressful.

The middle bit of the barn, with sliding metal doors and woodpile, is full of rubbish. There are trenches dug out with concrete rubble and plastic sacks with plastic bottles in, discarded buckets, containers and wiring, all strewn across the place. It's an absolute bloody pigsty, with no order. Paint tins and useless brushes. When we argue I think hotly – *Why is it such a mess? Why didn't more happen while he was out here? Was he reading Russian literature the whole time?*

And even as I write it, I know what has happened. He has dug out the trenches by hand – literally shovelling shit – so that we can build new foundations and new walls to support this building. He has done it on his own, year on year, while earning money to keep it all going – to pay for travel backwards and forwards to Britain, to try to hang on to his marriage and family. Which he has. But I'm still cross. It's still too bloody unconventional and totally bloody impossible.

The kids need a half-term break, to divide up the stretch of school life. I look at going by train to Redon and visiting Bea. The first time I tried driving there in the summer, I failed miserably on a misty and confusing road. I had to turn back, with two disappointed kids. I'll try harder this time.

James drives us to Vannes station and me and the kids travel on to Redon and spend a couple of days at Bea's house. Large, opulent, with shining woodwork and floors, clean smooth walls and paintwork. It's a big house, standing square in a complex of outbuildings. There are four bedrooms, two bathrooms… throws, rugs, beds, linen, lamps, hangings… She has been to Ikea and bought the lot, furnishing the house in one fell swoop.

There are textiles with outline leaf shapes – do you know the ones? Well, Bea has them. They form the tablecloth for her office desk, which is framed by the floor-to-ceiling windows and curtains. Their computers sit back-to-back at their desks in their shared office, with double doors to the kitchen and French windows to the front garden. It is all carefully constructed: even the throws have throws. The fireplace is large, and the wood is brought in using appropriately woven baskets. It is all highly tasteful, with large format books of topographical photographs featured on the glass coffee-table. Matching linen in the bedrooms, bedside lamps, towels, soap dishes.

Anna heads directly to the master bedroom and hooks up online. I don't know how many episodes of *Eastenders* she watches, but this is what she mainlines for the majority of our stay. Pierre, aged 5, is delightful. He speaks English with a delicious accent and is very small and sweet. His jumpers are homemade by his French granny – soft wool in muted brown, with trains and planes knitted in. We spend much of the first day painting a map of the world on a huge piece of cardboard, spread on the floor in the living room.

'We don't come in here much,' Bea says, and I wonder why on earth not, as I lie on the sofa with a book. And a throw. The light from the window is perfect to read by. The heat from the fire is just right. It is like Christmas, with Joe and Pierre mapping out the drawing, which Joe obligingly starts with South America. Later, Joe slopes off to a spot on the sofa and makes a start on YouTube, and Pierre and I take it in turns with the green and blue paint. My favourite is Greenland, which I paint white.

Martin spends his time at the computer in the office. Bea is outside, planting bulbs. Later, we go for a slow bike ride along the river Vilaine. It is flat and still, the fields nearby stubby with cut crops, the earth brown. I can imagine what it is like in February – like this, only frozen. We are on the plain; sometimes the river floods and Bea has seen photos of it coming to the basement door. When we get back from our ride she shows me all around the outbuildings, the small chicken and goat sheds, made of stone with quaint wooden doors. The large stone barn, taller than ours, is in better condition, the slate roof intact. The walls do not need pulling down. Bea runs me through her ideas for this space – the daydream of a large downstairs studio, with three bedrooms upstairs. Sounds familiar.

The second day we go swimming in Redon; half-term pool filled with half-term families. Like bobbing about in human soup, but with skullcaps on. Bea walks out in brown Spanish leather boots with 4-inch heels. When we come out of the pool, I notice I am wearing Joe's walking boots, leopard-print socks (thank you Mel) with jeggings and a shapeless top. It's not exactly manicured, but I don't mind, not really. Perhaps I should make more of an effort, it's true, and I won't team those particular items again.

The third day, we set off for home. James picks us up at Vannes station. He arrives wearing a canvas jacket, black T-shirt, stubble. He looks very handsome. He is kind and unfussy. We are very quiet on the way home. It is a little disorientating being back at the barn. I plant some bulbs and wait for the strangeness to pass.

I wonder out loud, talking to James from my bath later that evening. James is reading downstairs and Joe is flat on the bed next door, reading a magazine. There is a gold satin curtain on the bathroom opening, but you can hear everything within this space without doors. It makes conversation easier.

I lie up to my neck in the steam and ask what I think is a rhetorical question:

'I'm wondering – does having less money make you nicer?'

'What do you mean?' asks James.

'Being poor – does it make you more loving towards people?'

'An interesting idea,' he replies.

'I think it might do,' I say, swishing some bubbles about.

'Or bitter,' calls out Joe from the other room.

Your house sounds posh! I wrote to Bea, before we went.

Not posh – just Ikea! she wrote back. Same thing, I now think. Western eyes. Yes, of course Ikea is 'cheap' – but only if you have the money. There is a comfort and an ease that comes from money. Maybe that ease deepens a sense of entitlement, of surety. But also, perhaps born out of these same things, comes a sense of expectation, irritation, of boredom even.

I think of the article I've been reading online about the 'Ethics of Aesthetics' – a debate surrounding a highly saturated colour photograph of an African family outside their straw hut, staring straight into the camera.

Witnessing Bea's sense of urgency in the garden – planting all the bulbs before she jets off for another five weeks – inspires a similar sense in me.

Ah, I think to myself. *This is how you do it then. You have to* buy *all the things ready to plant them.*

So I go out with Anna and buy 100 tulip bulbs, a skimmia japonica, an escallonia, a half-price apple tree and a leylandii and continue digging along what will be my *barrière*. It *will* be my *barrière*. I wonder whether desperate English people buy and dig plants so as to make themselves happier, to make a stake for a happier time. I wonder if this is part of what planting is.

The evening turns sunny and calm. I am digging my excellent curved barrier, turning over the earth and letting my impressions work their way out of me. Monsieur Le Métayer – Ange – comes over. I try to explain what I am doing. I have mixed compost for the rhododendrons, but the ground is so stony, dry and poor – he can see that. He can also see the 10-metre trench I'm intending to dig and plant. It is marked by the kindling sticks that I laid out and Anna modified (in a better line, it has to be said).

We talk about the earth, the temperature, the weather. We have a similar circuitous conversation, most days.

Petit à petit! I say, drawing the conversation to a close, about to resume my digging.

Petit à petit l'oiseau fait son nid, he replies, his blue eyes twinkling in his crinkly brown face. Gesticulating round and round – a nest.

Ange = Angel.

And off he goes. I understand that saying and it strikes a chord and makes me feel much more peaceful. Then Ange turns and comes back. He wants me to know I can use the earth that lies in a big pile just over the track, on his land. It's a sort of dumping ground with weeds. I can't believe my luck – it is just what I have needed and at no cost. Let planting commence.

Pod Living

James was worn out and exhausted. A client had emailed to say his shutters were great but weren't stained well enough. He was supposed to go and collect them but had ground to a halt. I made him wake up and get up. I made him talk to me as we walked up the track and we did not argue, which was miraculous. He was miserable, saying that the thought of the day filled him with dread. I gave him a slight bollocking, and pointed out that if he wants to be solitary and spiritual, he should become a monk. He laughs at this, but I am serious. If he is going to continue as a self-employed businessman, he has to take the shit that comes with it – accountant, bank accounts, clients, emails and the like. He doesn't know whether he can 'toughen up' to fit the mould. James is very tough in lots of ways, but he is essentially a sensitive soul. The first thing he should do, I say, is put on a clean shirt and go and pick up those bloody shutters.

In one way, I hate James working for other people. I see it as a diversion from the real purpose here of building the barn. If we had enough money, I would like him to concentrate solely on the barn until it is done. But we don't have that… *luxury*, if that is the word. However, what we do have, as I pointedly tell him…

'Your bottom will get damp, like that,' he says.

I am sitting cross-legged on the track, where it curves at the top. Far enough from the barn that the kids cannot hear us.

'I don't fucking care,' I say. 'I have a period, and I Don't Fucking Care.'

I point out that what we are doing:

'Is a lot of people's dream. *Oh, I'd love to do up a barn in France,* they say. *Oh, I'd love to own my own business. It must be great to be a carpenter, and be able to do all the work yourself* and *save so much money.*'

The difference between lifestyles and ways of living, earning a living, are many and varied. I wonder sometimes about *whether it is actually possible* to earn and sustain a living in these circumstances and this particular situation. I think it is probably easier to work in the service industries, sit at a computer and live in a normal house, but even that isn't easy. I'm not sure how wealth is generated, because even normal folk are struggling, in the main (aren't they?), to pay the household bills and expenses. Those who are obviously not struggling, who have wealth – well-tended second homes for example – how have these folk got that money? Does it just come from being *very organised* and *looking after the pennies?* I know some people who have those qualities, and they struggle still. So it must be a combination of inherited wealth, good incomes, and shrewd money management. One of James's clients employs a mole-catcher. The detail of their lives must be extraordinary. The mole-catcher is for their sweet second home, specially renovated by James, with chestnut doors, staircases, windows and shutters.

I have a meeting tomorrow in the UK, a four-day worktrip, so I had better look my consultative best. The flight leaves Paris in a couple of hours. I have a room booked at the Holiday Inn. Imagine. A hotel room all to myself, with clean sheets and TV and high-speed internet... Blimey. I hope I can find my way around the town. I hope one day I'll actually get *paid*, because as ever this is all done on my astonishing overdraft.

One day I *will* get paid, and one day I *will* go the *Pépinière* in Bignan. On this trip I have to buy Anna a great many magazines, and Joe some Toblerone. It will be difficult for Anna in particular without me, I think. Joe was so bored this weekend that he went for several walks. I feel for them both, but am at a loss as to what to do. Having bedrooms will help. I don't know when they will be ready, but they will come. They will. This side of Christmas.

Paris airport, with a four-hour wait until the flight to Cardiff. The weather in Paris is wet and grey. The sandwiches cost £5.80. It gives me time to think about Working for Others: I don't believe this is the way to make money. I did think that if you worked hard you would get your reward – stoicism, I think it's called. But I don't know whether I still believe that. I think it is worth spending time *on your own thing*, more so than *on other people's thing*.

As it is, the pod-home we are building within the barn is developing. We moved into Anna's room. It is a little like being a rabbit in a hutch – we are all in there, lined up on our mattresses, side by side. It just fits the four of us. One wall is painted 'jazzy purple'. Anna took such immense pleasure in painting it, it is a shame she has to wait until we have moved ourselves out of there before she can make it fully her own.

This first bedroom is made of sheets of 8 x 4 plywood, well insulated with Kingspan. It's like a box, suspended above what I shall call the hallway. The hallway is the main entrance area as you come in the big back door. It has shelves of cut logs and kindling, with a narrow wooden ladder up to the 'attic' and a door to the kitchen/living area. The bathroom and Bedroom 1 are lit by a single glass rooftile. They are old, and difficult to find, these *tuiles de verre*.

Large metal doors open to the front of the building. When these are open the light streams in; the doorway then frames the formal elegance of the oak trees on Ange's lawn. To the right of these metal doors is a small corridor to the workshop. All these interior walls are made of construction or 'shuttering' ply. Some are insulated and some are not, yet. I am dying to paint the kitchen wall white and hang our coats on it, and have a rack for all our boots and shoes. All this will have to wait until the bedrooms are done. All of us need some private space.

When I first arrived I wanted to put up a lightshade and shelves in the kitchen, to house all our stuff. James said not to, because he wanted to insulate the outside of the kitchen wall. The one with the sink, fridge, washing machine, cooker and work surface on. The kitchen, in other words, needs to be taken away from the wall, the wall insulated and clad, and then everything put back again. *Then* we can put up the ceiling, paint it, hang lights etc.

I feel my impulses squashed. It makes me sad, because I feel there is nothing I can do, practically, to improve our surroundings – I have to wait.

'What can I do then?' I ask.

'Well, there is plenty to do outside,' he says.

This is true. It is also good for me. Pulling weeds, throwing rocks, realising and satisfying the unfulfilled need I've had for many years, to heal a childhood self that was happy playing in the woods, alone. Whatever happens, I believe it has done that. I have my own space to gawp, and think, and pull harsh brambles for the bonfire.

When we talked recently, James mentioned how his excitement has gone out of things. He used to enjoy the creative energy of embarking on a job. He says the only thing that keeps him going now is his perfectionism, but he recognises that this 'might also be the thing that kills me.'

I can see how the perfectionism is necessary – to get things right, otherwise things do not work and the same job needs doing again. I have absolutely no idea how he does things like plumbing and electrics and building. I have to like perfectionism, but at the same time I find it very frustrating, it will not be hurried. Where the barn is concerned, I have to go with how James decides it – there is a process to the progress.

Flying over London, I catch the tail end of the Thames snaking in the night-time. Orange clouds of light, hanging at odd perspectives from the plane window. I think, *if the plane plummets, I feel alright.* Cardiff hung with lights. Hotel sheets, the loneliness that comes with hotel rooms. Bath. Bubbles. See myself in a full length mirror again. I still look slimmer; it would be good to wear clothes that followed my body now. Taxi journeys in city streets, my voice loud and strange in my ears. Words loose and new.

'I live in France; I am a consultant.'

It is the first time I've said them out loud, to people. I test the words in my mouth. Every time I have to say them, I am always surprised. Taxi drivers, lots of them. Colleagues at dinner, intrigued by language, culture and kids' education. Think I'm daft, a few of them. Romantically crazy.

'But how are you earning money?' Jonathan asks.

'Well, I'm working,' I reply.

They are older men, mainly, who own houses themselves in France. The sort of houses that feature on the covers of architecture magazines.

Meetings, talk that goes around in circles with powerful women. You can hear the air crackle as chemical waves of ambition and disdain battle it out before subsiding. Lack of decision, confusion. I keep my counsel, staying quiet so that they don't realise my lack of insight. Does everyone feel they are a fraud?

Back home, long journey. Paris connections and weary nights in hotel not-sleeping.

The kids look taller, composed when they come to pick me up. James looks scruffy in work clothes but keeps the children well with good food and humour. He looks tired, pale beneath the eyes. It takes me a few days to catch up, only now do I feel a balance restoring. The day is fresh and birds sing. Mushrooms jumping up, mustard-yellow flowers in the field. I have Hoovered and mopped and changed the sheets, which means I can rest now.

I think James is under critical stress conditions. The scrappiness and brown-ness of the barn gets to me slightly, not in a crescendo, but in a quiet, ever-so-tired way. I'm not sure if this is because I've just been used to more sophisticated surroundings (hotel, offices) or simply a response to November leaves, grey stillness and the odour of pigshit, which hangs in the air some mornings like grease, unmoving. There is so much to do – our circumstances and situation are still so basic. I see it through others' eyes when Granny and Grandpa come. They are staying in a *gîte* nearby for two weeks. We only have this kitchen pod-room for us all to sit in, though the caravan comes into its own, then.

And yet: I loved the stillness last night, as we were seeing them off, the moon behind a swirl of cloud. We are a tight unit, the four of us, safe in our shared bedroom. We all four of us understand what it is to live like this, it is a shared knowledge. I love the oaks, grand and unmoving, whose roots run right under my feet. The damp, light, and fresh air, all for the taking. I imagine more plants softening the edges of the building. I imagine sunny days, when people come and it is easier.

Anna seems happy at school. She eats breakfast now. It is the last day of the week today, so we will go and visit Granny and Grandpa in their *gîte* this evening. They chat about TV programmes and I wonder if that is not an easier way to live. Like Susie up the road, with *Cash in The Attic* on Sky in the middle of the day, and ski-ing for Christmas. Here, James has just received his copy of *The Spiritual Crisis of Man.*

I do think that I understand him, though. I understand the need to make a home from scratch, and I believe that this period of time is about putting the same amount of work into a house as we did in Wales, in order to turn that terrace house from a shell into a home.

Kids visiting *gîte* with grandparents. Driving through Pontivy – everything shut except NOZ – and Netto. Strange wandering vagrants clustering around islands of cheapness. Jardiland a bliss of rabbits and fish and plastic pink flamingos. Quiet at the barn. Bedroom to ourselves. Still, damp and misty weather. Mushrooms coming up like gifts. Clearing slimy black wood and brambles onto the bonfire.

Gîte complex owned and run by people from Manchester called Rachel and Simon. Must make a packet in high season, but quiet and hollow yesterday. Rachel tells me the story about the TV company that wanted to make a feature out of them, until they saw their business plan and realised they had accounted for every eventuality.

'They were looking more for people who had come over with just 2,000 euros in the bank – that sort of thing,' she says. 'Things which were more likely to fail – the tensions would make better TV.'

'Oh yeah?' I say.

Blimey.

Anna unhappy at school. When I picked her up on Wednesday and asked how she was she said, 'Fed up and a bit lonely all the time.'

I feel the same old protective fierceness and my instinct is to take her out of school, get her intensive private French tuition. Probably what we both need. I know the only way through this is to learn the language.

It's sunny. Mushroom soup, mushroom land. Dried mushrooms. I'm just doing the work that is in front of me; I will make some dinner later and try to remain calm and keep my eye on the ball. It is pretty grim on the whole.

Granny and Grandpa try to make it better; talking about gardens and having tea and lemoncake in the sun helps. Anna seems happier, more put-together, today. Joe is practising his climbing knots. James is silent; he says he can't talk 'until all this is done', pointing upstairs to the rooms. He might be able to speak about Christmas time.

Continually surprising, the sea-changes in moods and attitude. Such a difficult week, then yesterday woke like a dream. Sunshine, lizards, blackbirds, ladybirds, *boeuf bourguignon* (not containing those things) chocolates, cider. All because of the sunshine. My birthday. Today spent painting

Bedroom 2, shining the torch as James wires up the lights. It all seems possible again.

The contrasts: two sides to the same coin. The delicate balance that can shift from day to day. The stench, like an olfactory layer of filth, that hangs, stuck to the atmosphere, cloaking the day which lies still and flat. Colour, the fragrant waves of yellow flowers on the mustard plants, acres of new growth, green, acid-yellow over the brow of the hill and alongside the track. So tenuous you can only just catch the scent, and when I do, I breathe great gulps of it.

The field and sky marrying in tone and luxury. A silky weave, a gauze of air and light, the violet blue sky over Guénin hill. Ancient hill, a gentle mound some 6km away, 'where the English live' but also the site of Druid 'offerings', apparently.

That colour, that light, those sensations, continue to bind me to this place. The small oak trees, tiny seedlings sprouted all over the ground from where we scattered the acorns in August. I think of transplanting these youngsters along the perimeter of the land. They will take aeons to grow, but as Granny points out, I am 'impatient' in my planting, and that once these plants are established too close together, I will regret it.

Bedrooms are complete – how quickly we nest and cosy them. Anna went to town on the purple and pink theme and I followed her lead in my room, by arranging bags hanging on the painted board. Old rugs that have lived in other spaces now spread on our floor. We need new rugs, new lampshades, some chairs and a bed for Joe.

Prettying upstairs has revolutionised me. I veer between wondering how the fuck we are ever going to afford to actually make this into a house, with things like floor tiles and walls, to cleaning the top kitchen shelf and arranging pots. James is very obliging, drilling holes. We are making a better office area. I have a Hoover upstairs plus a Hoover downstairs – this makes me very happy. I want to mop, but don't have time before I pick up Joe…

Or do I…? I am domestic. I delight in clean order, within our pod-home.

Outside, I took the old beams from under the wood pile and arranged for a veg plot, then changed my mind and moved them over to form a solid line for my *barriere*. I think it will work, when planted up. It gives a distinct perimeter, a definite edge, which it probably needed. There is still lots of digging and planting to be done. I need to email my mum and warn her that this is poor, that she may be shocked when she visits at Christmas. I uprooted the rhododendrons and moved them closer to the main bare area of my *barriere*. I arranged them in more of a cluster and gave them good compost. The rootball I dig up is just the same as when I planted it: the white tendrils have not set about extending yet. They remind me of me, of us, and how we might be.

These pod-rooms, our bedrooms. How they have changed and improved our living. Now when Joe comes home from school, he bounces upstairs to his space and plays footy on his Xbox, lying on the foam mattress on the floor. His space is separated from ours by a thick red velvet curtain that is only partly eaten by mice. Anna's bedroom is along the landing. She has decorated her room and lies on her bed watching her netbook screen. She has used an old wooden desk to house all her school books. She is happy with the organisation. I am happy with the organisation. James has done what he said he would, and continues to.

The weather gets colder, the fire is all-important, our little steam engine that he lights early in the morning, a half-hour before me and the kids get up. He works hard, always works hard. We need to keep moving with it, I know: at some point the novelty of our pod-rooms will wear off. They are dark – I need to source glass tiles. The rooms are all decorated with our things – this seems to be one of the biggest changes. Some of that disparate stuff lying in the attic gets dusted down and placed in a room: housed. This includes my hamper of clothes. Now all our clothes are in *cupboards* in *rooms*. This is progress. I want to nail the Map of the World on Joe's wall, and dry the throw to hang his side of the curtain wall.

It all seems possible when Michel calls round one evening with news that Joe has been nominated 'outstanding student' by the teaching committee. He has a Distinction, but '*Shh!*' – he puts his finger to his lips – we are not to know yet. It seems possible when Pluméliau lights are being rigged up and I am looking forward, shyly, to the Christmas market. It seems possible, if I am able to continue to work freelance, with occasional trips back to Britain. It seems possible that we can be successful financially, when we have no major overheads here and have work coming in, as it is now.

I lie in bed this evening deliciously early, reading *Women who Run with the Wolves,* next to James reading his book. Side by side, the kids nearby. James reads a book on Meditation, this a week after he told me he was giving up *Spirituality for Materialism*. He can't help himself. He said the meditation book had turned up at the wrong time – we ordered the book weeks ago and had given up on it when it finally arrived.

'Perhaps the book found me,' he says.

'Now is not the time for meditation,' I say.

I am frightened he will retreat to silence and solitude and there is *so much to do*. I am all too aware of the scale of this project. And then I think, after all, if there is ever a place and time to meditate, surely it is here, now.

River

Mr Rufus gets Day 1 of his advent calendar.

Yesterday Anna and I mosied around Remungol, looking for a bleedin' *pépinière*, and on to Guénin. Driving around, stumbling across all sorts of houses – houses with moats and lakes, polytunnels and caravans, palm trees and chicken houses. We found ourselves on a road that simply petered out. Down a steep hill, a renovated house stood ghostly and abandoned, the conifers flagging in the undergrowth. I was glad to get back up that hill, past the fancy BMW and the obvious *gîtes*, past the little dogs play-barking in the road.

'Why didn't you buy a barn like that?' Anna asked, of the spooky big house by the river. 'At least it has a roof, and nice stones.'

Practical child. Good point.

We find our bearings, drive a wide triangle between Guénin, Locminé and Baud. We find the *patisserie* open and buy chocolate pastries. We see the poster for the Christmas market again, jewel-like greens and golds. I feel deflated from seeing all these renovations that are obviously in so much better condition than ours.

Why did we have to buy a dud?

It will take us 15 years to un-dud it.

It is strange, how my mood can go from so optimistic, digging in the damp sunshine this morning, to disconsolancy. I do some more digging when we get back, to rebalance me. James helps Anna with her SVT homework (*Sciences de la Vie et de la Terre*) about animals and whether they are herbivores or omnivores. I move dark leafmould like chocolate velvet from one side of the garden to the other. It all happens very slowly. I dig it in.

This morning, James struggling, we walk up the track a little and then take an alternate route, down through the trees along the river. The ground is thick with copper leaves and all sorts of fungi disintegrating in the rain. Red and white, fly agaric… It would have been in its prime a couple of weeks ago. The air is clear and fine, rich with the scent of freshness. I take deep lungfuls, and when we come to a clearing opening onto the river, I do some sun salutations.

There are large rocks of quartz in the slow-moving river. It is shallow to cross, deeper downstream. It will be good to swim in on a summer's day. The water is lively, not like the sluggish dead-rat water further upstream – this is different. There are many oak leaves stacked horizontally in the water, Goldsworthy-esque. It reminds me how much time I used to spend wandering around, playing with such things. I wade over to the other side, see the island, and wade back.

It is highly unusual for us to spend time in this way and it provokes a conversation we wouldn't normally have. It does us good to get away from the barn, to see that there is something else going on. We talk about the balance of things, about work and pressure and well-being. It is important that he sees his circumstances objectively. Seeing him in the woods reminds me how he and I used to be, in the beginning. It rains hard, we come home for lunch, our conversation has been so expansive we are quiet now, a little absorbed and unsure where it goes next. I feel fine, quiet and steady and waiting for my colleague Siân to ring for the next phase of this work. There is an element of healing in this. Remembering through walking how I *used* to feel, how we *used* to feel, the freedom of possibility in walking all day.

On occasions throughout the day I get a painting from the attic, or tack up a poster for Joe, bringing things out that haven't been seen for a while – our old things that made up our old home. It seems like such a long time ago now, Trefriw and the river, Mynydd and the rain. Trefriw and the floods, the steep hill. So much water.

The things I tack up are: a green and blue tie-dye *fleur-de-lis* throw, that I bought in Swiss Cottage before Joe was born. I was never sure of it, but it covered my single bed back then. It hangs on his side of the divide, and works quite well I think: the motif fitting the idea of flags and castles. I pin up the map of the world on the pitched ceiling.

I bring down a clutch of paintings from the attic, dust them off then take some back up again. I don't want old paintings, of my own or others'. Bernard's small off-hand oil should be the most expensive of course, but it is not a good painting. Viv's pastel fruitbowl, impressionistic fuzzy grapes, sweet and familiar, but too familiar for now. So those two paintings go back up to the attic and lie one on top of the other. The two people who made those pictures used to be married. They are getting older now, one is a well-known painter and the other has just started showing her work properly. All these juxtapositions.

The paintings that go up on the walls are paintings that have not been hung before. That sounds very grand, for this little space. They are an unmounted mandala print and an unmounted abstract ink/stitch piece, both by two of last year's students. Gwyn's small framed print will hang somewhere and the Hirsty 'dots' will too, though James is 'not bothered' about that. Small things. Small things become big things, when you see them day in, day out, so often. My nana's old wooden cutlery drawer I have washed out and will use as a novelty shelf, when it is dry.

Ah yes, the novelty shelf is tiny, and filled with tiny things; a children's teaparty scale. It is interesting how things shrink to fit, like Alice after having drunk the liquid. It is novel, placing things, moving things around, in a confined space. Today is a beautiful sharp and sunny day. I spend most of it in the semi-dark at the computer, but step out occasionally for quick walks up the track. I ask James to take a break from the workshop and come with me as I think he needs the air and light too, these short December days.

We walk briefly down to the river again. It is different this time, but still a novelty to be walking with him, just for the sake of walking. The river is so much fuller today. It was a full moon last night with plenty of water, so all those Goldsworthy leaves have completely gone, the water much higher and browner and no chance of walking across to the island. I think Joe would like this bit of river, the island and benign, climbable branches.

It is colder now. When we open the door from the kitchen to the hallway, to take the eternal teabags to the bin, for instance, or out to the loo, the difference in temperature is marked. Part of this winter will be about keeping good – or just even – tempered, living in such close confines with dark evenings. The kids chatter at the dinner table. Friday night is pizza night, and James has done loads today; worked, made lunch, made dough, picked up kids, done shopping, while I have been glued to the machine.

I made him throw away a thin old jumper, which smelled of caravan.

'That's because it's been stored in there for the past five years.'

I gave him his Christmas present (black thermals) early. And now I'm going to browse for a proper chunky jumper for him, something nice for me to rest my head on.

Kids at school, James at work. Washing on line. Work on go. Done the shopping – chicken, milk, apples. Eat a cheese baguette standing up gawping out the window. Wonder whether it is better to be poor in France, rather than Britain, after all.

Yesterday we went to the sculpture park, and although Anna stayed in the car it was a Family Excursion and this is a New Thing and a Good Idea. Saturday night Anna and I bought the Christmas tree. We got a letter from the school with *Félicitations* and *Encouragement* from the school council. Joe has got a new wooden bed made by dad and a brand new mattress. Joe and I went for a walk in the Sunday afternoon rain, along the river to the boulders and island, me taking us down the wrong track with brambles, him marching to 'a marching song'. The water subsided again, still fast but lower so I could wade over to the island in my wellies. Joe hoiked up his jeans and came too, walking boots wet through. Walked fast back up the hill, him jogging and me gasping as he pushed me on.

'Out of shape, Mum,' he said.

And he was right.

I walk along the river, lay my hands hot and florid against the thick green moss of the tree-trunk, trying to let my hectic mind and heat into the tree, trying to draw some of the cool of the tree into me. Fragmented mind, strange dreams. The river flowing through a still landscape, trees tall and formal. Small yellow and lime-green leaves still hanging to the branches, drops of rain along their edges. Orange and purple underfoot, thick and brown sodden leaves. The river running through is the only movement, apart from the occasional swoop of birds from the large stick nests, up high.

The wind is blowing leaves past the kitchen window, left to right across the rectangular pane. Joe is upstairs with two lumps in his neck – I had to pick him up from school. His skull hurts and his glands are up. Anna is fine and cheerful.

James has been clearing rubbish out of the middle section, not wanting to run workshop machinery because of Joe's headache. He has just taken some stuff to the tip – it is very good to get rid of stuff: detritus and accumulated crap from the last five years. Real dirty rubbish – leftovers of wood, plastic, metal…

It makes James feel awful, this clearing – not least because he 'can't see an end to it'.

But we have not yet even begun, I feel like telling him.

'Can you see an end to it?' he asks.

'Well, yes, I can see something in my mind's eye.'

I have to, because we need to move away from sleeping cheek by jowl. The kids will need their own proper space, we will need real rooms at some point in the not-too-distant future. But I tell him I am not the one who is physically doing this, so it is easy for me to see how and what needs to be done, sitting here on my arse by the warm fire, at the computer.

I tell him to look at 'the problem' objectively, without emotion. Easy to say. I also tell him that of course he feels miserable doing this; he has not seen sunlight properly for a couple of days – it is the darkest time of year and the work itself is horrible – dirty, in the true sense of the word.

'Objectivity is good,' I say. 'Otherwise everything gets tangled up; emotions, money, time, commitments and priorities.' We try to untangle it.

We discuss focusing solely on the barn, James not working for clients. We have been through all these ideas before, but I'm still trying to arrange them in my mind. I tell James I think it may be necessary to borrow money to renovate the barn, in one way or another.

I think building a real house out of a barn is probably a life's work. If you want to see an end in sight, you need to work on it continuously, and quickly. In order to do that, you need money; to buy materials and to allow you the time to focus on building, rather than working for other folk. In order to borrow money, you need to show that you have an income allowing you to make the loan repayments. If you get an English mortgage on a French renovation, the money comes through in stages. You need to provide a plan of when work will be done, and they need to check that the work is at a certain stage before they release the next part.

I would borrow £30,000 with the idea of giving ourselves a year to 16 months to build the barn. I think it will take twice that, and more. But for it to get done, properly, with walls, roof, windows, doors, toilet, kitchen, lighting, I would focus on it solely.

We do not want to borrow any money, so that leaves only a few different options.

Either: Carry on as we are, trying to do work on the barn while working for other people.

Or: Sell it. It's not worth very much at the moment, and we will feel as though we have failed.

The important thing, I think, is to disassociate the emotional side from the practical, working, building, financial side. To get this house built at all requires James's skill, expertise and commitment. That he is a French-registered Artisan is great, because anything we spend on the barn is TVA (VAT) reclaimable. Also, if we should ever decide to get a loan to pay for it, we can 'employ' James to work on it, so the money we borrow goes straight back in to our pot, if you like. Theoretically, in that scenario, the money I earn pays off the loan which is paying him to work on the barn. I think that sounds like a reasonable sort of plan, but it relies on me being able to earn the sort of money that can pay back a loan, which I don't, at the moment. It would also mean jumping through hoops in order to secure a loan – paperwork and more paperwork. Could be done though, I think.

Over the following days we talk over and around the above. It is almost impossible to have a private conversation, as the kids are always around and we are all in such close proximity. Joe is still off school with a swollen neck and on horrible antibiotics. Thank God he has a bed and a room, of sorts. James, still not running machinery, has been chipping off the old plaster in the middle barn.

'Like Middle Earth,' I say to Anna.

'Yeah, right.'

Removing the plaster in the middle room reveals splendid dressed stone – good stone, which James likes. He stands in the barn in the halflight with his small pickaxe slung over his shoulder and looks perfectly in his element, pointing out how the walls could be positioned, to give structural strength and make a nice shape. This is the room which has now been cleared of all that rubbish. The rubble of ancient plaster is all around us, green-grey with aged slime. It is good to see the stonework. It is even better to hear that the walls of middle barn are straight, and need not come down. I imagine it with windows and a stove.

I walk along the river on Sunday morning, think about the thread of the river all the way down to the sea, hear the birdcall cut through the mist, those straight trees again, gunshot echoing in the distance. Walking down the track in the early mist another morning two deer saw me, on their way across the field; archetypal silhouettes. We stood and looked at each other for a while, then they jounced back the way they'd come, into the small woods.

The full moon hung straight through the rectangle of our kitchen window the other morning, large yellow circle suspended just for us. This morning the moon was clear in a dark sky; it's darker later in the mornings here. I have made pumpkin pie, am making Georgian chicken and am drying the washing. I wonder whether Nana had it right, after all: a daily routine of simply buying and preparing food. As James points out, that is what Women's Lib was all about changing. I have not forgotten that, but it is a novelty to spend all day on a Monday cooking, then a little light digging in the sunshine, the wind colder now.

I got a message from Dave, a colleague, the other day: *Are you managing to get any of your own work done?*

Bugger all, I replied. He meant design, or painting perhaps. I didn't go on to say that I didn't *feel* like doing 'my own work'. *This* is my own work – digging and trying to make this barn a home. I don't feel a need to make paintings or sell paintings. Seeing James in the middle barn the other day made me think that it is really a big sculpture.

Apron

I really haven't laid it on regarding today's pumpkin pie.

I *made* (by hand) *short crust pastry*, following Nigella's bleedin' recipe, and *baked it blind*. Bought several recipe items from Pluméliau intermarché (they didn't have dried soured cherries, Nigella), chopped up some of the monstrous child-proportioned pumpkin which Ange keeps giving us. Chop chop mix blend, yuck orange stringy pulp take a detour on the recipe… regret, will it work? Too much liquid, oh it has set, washing up, oven, check, wash up etc etc, thinking: *Fuck me I have been in the kitchen for over two hours with this orange mush that I'm not even sure I like… why don't people just buy one? Well, we know why, don't we folks.*

I just need to have got that off my chest. Now I have stuffed a chicken with the addition of *pine nuts* instead of fucking cherries, and all seems well. We are going to have a mini feast tonight, in honour of Anna, who got a Good report and who I love mostly muchly absolutely, although she only ate the following this weekend:

- pizza
- hotdog
- meringue
- cake
- bread

And although I had to make a special journey to the shop to buy the bloody pizza, she wandered around in the rain outside the caravan, brolly up, book in hand, reciting what she has to memorise for maths. And I love her because she is glamorous, watches Hollywood DVDs with me in the caravan, with cookies tight against the grey Sunday afternoon. Because of those things, and also because I want to get some vegetables down 'er. And me. We eat too many biscuits. Gotta get with the grapes.

Oh yeah, and, while we're at it, I want to have a middle barn room, with windows and doors and stairs, but mainly windows that I can look out of, and put a geranium in a pot, on the windowsill, facing out east down to our neighbours. Facing out. Dressed stone.

And a stove, with positioned red-enamel kettle, just where those small recesses are. The stone cleaned up, and the stove independent – no soot – streamlined, warm, and light. It is a good thing to see in your mind's eye. Keeps you going.

James has rethought his approach, he tells me. We may not have an interior cavity wall, but simply use those that are already standing, where they are structurally sound. He is pleased to be taking down the small end barn and has shifted the floorboards that were open to the sky. He likes the stone, it is 'a treasure' to him. He intends to use it on the block-built workshop front, ultimately, to make it visually cohesive. Imagine.

There is nothing redeeming about the day. The wind is gusting in a grey sky. I sit close to the stove, which is doing its steam-train thing and making a whistling, drawing noise, belting out the heat. All the colour has drained from the oaks, from the grass, from the branches. Not even the mustard is yellow. It's winter. The last few days have been stormy, with strong winds blowing branches down in the night. The electricity went off in the darkness and I paralysed myself with fear that it would be off for days; how would I explain to EDF that our 'leccy was off? Feverish imaginings, only to find the lights working as usual in the morning.

It has been stormy, then very still, then stormy again, and I'm struggling to keep on top of it. I need to wear tights under my trousers, and toughen up. I need to go out for a walk in it, perhaps along the river. It does not entice me. Joe is still unwell in bed; he finished the last of the antibiotics last night.

Going out of the door into the hall-pod is *raw*, with the steel front doors open, blowing in old leaves. There are clumps of mud around from where they have dropped off James. He is chipping away at the walls. We don't speak much, both a bit drawn. He must be itching to start the machines to get on with work, but Joe sleeps on …

Yesterday we went to L'Orient, on our long-planned Christmas shopping trip. The thunder, wind and lightning blew us along the packed roads, lights bright against the heavy rain. L'Orient is a sprawl of out-of-town furniture stores, the centre a complicated mass of intersections. We found a spot and parked, walking along the harbour with the tall yachts clanking against their moorings. People-watching – women in boots and skirts, tailored jackets. H&M an emporium of high-priced clothes – I thought it was supposed to be cheap? Anna and I spend an hour in the shop, sweltering in our coats and scarves, while Anna tries on clothes. At the changing rooms a long snake of queuing, pissed-off looking French women. We take our place in the queue for the till, behind glossy women with manicured hair, face, bag, boots and jacket. Co-ordinated. Caramel and black. Sheer tights, sheer hair, sheer makeup. Matching purse and boots. Patent leather bag.

I feel old and unkempt. My trousers have developed a patina with age, and the corduroy has lost its shape. They are five years old. My red boots are from a different time, a different me – a bouncy, feisty me that directed art students around the studios and could wear mid-calf red boots with tight jeans. Can't do that over 40. My boots are six years old, the zip is only just holding together on the left side and there is a rime of saltwater white on the toe. The top half of me is better – Anna even compliments me on it; fur muff, sunglasses, black reefer coat and lipstick. She thinks that's okay, and tells me so as we walk past those boats and the funfair in the wind. And we are all together, I think, walking behind James and Joe along the busy pavement. We are all in this together.

But my fur snood and black coat do not match, I do not *co-ordinate*.

This is not how it should be. How did this happen? How do I rectify it?

The mass and volume and speed and cost in the shop is depressing. I spend money I don't have, my only consolation that Anna's clothes are functional, warm and pretty. Am I compensating for our rough living by buying luxury things I cannot afford? Why do all my clothes seem unsuitable, when they suited me well enough before? Should I actually *buy* the things that might cure my wardrobe-*malaise*, using money I don't have, or make do with tights and clobber and stick it all together; wear my itchy red pullover for Christmas?

I am going to Try Harder; fish out some clothes other than the ones I've been wearing, make sure I am warm and barn-worthy. I'm going to buy ingredients for a meal and cook it and keep us healthy in this wintry time. The winter is going to get harder, and I will need strategies to cope. Having an impenetrable layer of clothing is a good start.

Word of the day – *l'orageux*.

Glamour Tips for Barn Living:

Wear a muff. A fur snood. Makeup, even if you are not intending to go anywhere and the nearest neighbours are the pigs.

I put on makeup and tights and an extra coat, wellies. I head out of the barn into the day. Three hunters stand still on the track, their dogs a carousel of frantic yelps. Men with caps on, rifles hooked over their arms, walking slowly across the field. I feel like shouting, 'Get off my land!' But of course, I don't know it, in French.

Joe still ill, machines still off. Went and found James removing stones, one by one, from the end barn, the oldest part. The wall gap-toothed, the first beam coming down. Orange clay soil underneath. The foundations to the barn are big lumps of quartz. I like that. The other day when I was shifting some quartz to encircle a small oak, I remembered the games mum would make when I was a kid – day-long fantasies involving small white pebbles as magic stones, or fairy sweets. Dressing up with friends and wandering around fields.

James moves the stones into different piles; he will lower the height of the wall all around, then create an opening through which we can wheelbarrow stones. I can help with that. Today I just stand and watch, pleased that I am not freezing bloody cold and feel somewhat like myself again. He is strong and lean, slowly and surely the building is coming down. There is daylight there now: all the old floorboards have gone. There are many more beams remaining, some of which he will re-use. He reckons they're about 200 years old. I put on *Brun Orne* Bourjois lipstick and my fur snood and head to Leclerc.

On the last day of school before Christmas, what should be a delightful day turns into a bit of a quest. Wind has been blowing a storm all night. The road this morning was strewn with parts of fallen trees, the road a carpet of twiggy greenery. I go back to bed after dropping off Anna, but sleep doesn't come. Joe wakes up and has a livid red rash all over his body. I make an emergency appointment with Dr Duno, who I am pissed-off with because his batch of medicines was ineffectual. I am also pissed-off as I don't know how to explain I'm pissed-off in French. The secretary sighs at my inadequacy and lack of understanding. Oh, okay, *onzeheuresetdemie*. I get it.

I put on my armour before heading out. Purple, 'it's nearly Christmas', jumper and makeup. We drive to the Doctor's, Joe's face a hotchpotch of red spots. He feels selfconscious and uncomfortable. We pass the big chestnut that has come down in the night. The doctor prescribes more tablets to cope with the allergic reaction Joe's had to the antibiotics. I hand over the money.

We go to the chemist. I hand over more money and become embroiled in more poor French. The medic speaks to Joe in French and to me in English. We come home. I am exhausted and demoralised and the fire is out. But we're all in one piece. Joe is in good humour and has a baguette and a cola on the way home in the car. I mis-pronounce everything – can't even get *jambon* right. I feel disenchanted, anxious and accusatory. Why haven't we got proper health cover sorted out? This must be my Number 1 Priority.

I'm still learning about the Health System, trying to work it out. You pay *Cotisations*, a form of National Insurance. Then, when you go to the Doctor's, you pay him up front, for being looked at. Then you go to the pharmacy and pay for the medicines the doctor has prescribed. You then fill in a form to have the monies reimbursed – the *mutuelle* (insurance) covers that part of it. I am sure it is simple and makes perfect sense for people who have grown up in the system, but to me it seems *unwieldy*, in terms of paperwork.

'Why does it have to be so fucking *difficult*, with brown forms and bloody stickers?' I let off steam describing my morning to James.

The satellite internet is down, we think the satellite dish has moved in the storm. We ring Bart who says more strong weather is forecast tonight, so to ring tomorrow, when perhaps it might have righted itself. I walk up the track and finally get the emails downloaded to my phone. It is damn cold out there, the wind strong and mean. I fantasise about safe terraced houses, with comfy sofas and constant TV. Why want anything more?

At least we have power.

At least Joe's rash is recognisable and understandable.

At least we are warm and clean and dry.

Last night, playing chess by the fire, dark and stormy outside, there was the terrible scream of pigs being taken away by the trucks. It was so gruesome in the desolate night that we had to laugh.

The leaves on the path have a slush of crushed ice. James and I walked along by the river and the flood: black leaves trailing in high water. Sun glare, bouncing rays right back at me. I could have stayed there all day in that spot. I imagine the fast water carrying away all the fragments of yuck that are left in me. I had an attack of palpitations the other day, walking up the track. It happens sometimes, when I am over-tired, viral, under stress, or all three.

I took the kids to Vannes and met Bea. We walked through the narrow alleyways gazing in the *chic* shop windows. The kids had *barbe à papa* on the harbour and went on the merry-go-round. They will stay with Bea for a couple of days, until Christmas Eve, along with my mum and Charles who are visiting for two weeks. They need the break away from the barn, and I need the break, I realise, driving back. I miss the kids already, but Joe has very kindly left me little pockets of old socks in unexpected places.

I Hoover and tidy, write a swift article on the sculpture park. A bit of work, then the river for a 4pm walk; all timetables different without children. Eerily still. No birdsong, at least not for a little while, then it comes like tropical squawking. Burrs, those nests up in the tall thin poplars are not nests at all; they are growths, like *filigree* condensed cobwebs, like Dr Zeuss illustrations on strange unworldly moors. They form spheres up there, like student drawings for contemporary light features. I love them, I want to take a photograph of them, on the poplars planted so formal and straight, right up to the river's edge. I stand in the field that I still dare not cross, and look at the pale mauvey grey of the trees. A fish jumps and makes me cry out in surprise. The water is viscous, a curious muddy green.

This wood undergrowth is the same as the Manet painting: the picnic in the trees. So overgrown it could spook you, if you weren't a tough grown-up lady like me. The rime from floodwater leaves a grey sludge over the track. Some *citron* yellow and lime leaves are still hanging on in there; they float down and one lands right in my hand.

Washing out, washing in. Rainy day, some wrapping of presents. Looking at tax returns and health insurance agents online. Laughably expensive. I think the world runs on insurance. At least we have up-to-date European Health Insurance cards now, but otherwise still nothing else. The annual and monthly fees of private health insurance are absurd. BUPA is £4472 to cover us all for the year. Not going to happen.

James and I did the Christmas shopping. We spent eight hours in and out of high-end Pontivy joints like Aldi, Lidl, NOZ, Leclerc. Even though we were careful and even though we didn't really buy anything fab (two panettone and a basket of clementines, some non-alcohol pop for me and Michel at New Year, some extremely dodgy and cheap fizz for Bea), despite all that, we still spent 190E.

My New Year's resolutions may be vast this year. It may be that I decide to Commit to this, push all duality aside and embrace my new life. It may be that I decide to Nullify all Negativity, brush all chips off shoulders, and look to the new, with trust and optimism.

I need to learn how to have things to hand that Anna will eat without protestation and without her beautiful fangs falling out. Cheese on toast, for example. For that 'just arrived home from school what-is-there-to-eat?' crisis point. *Healthy Eating for Preteens*. Gotta look it up on Google. Pissing down outside.

Tomorrow I will drive to Beyond Redon, to collect the kids and bring them home for Christmas. I am scared, but optimistic. Have to do it, anyway, so makes no odds if I'm bloody scared or not. I aim for it to be mildly enjoyable, tootling along semi-deserted roads that aren't too wiggly. I'm taking the back-road route, the yellow line that runs west to east.

In the event, James drove us down to Bea's. We went the back roads, and it was pretty and quaint, with a church at the centre of every small town. It was pretty evident that something was wrong with Anna when we arrived. She was pale and drawn, with dark eyes – she had been crying, Joe said. He had a terrible hacking cough. We exchanged gifts and hugs and the day was convivial and sunny. On the drive home Anna said not a word, and when we arrived back at the barn she went straight to bed and drew the covers over her head.

Christmas day at the barn was a routine of meal and gifts. Joe really saved the day, refusing to open anything until Anna was present. His spirit and general goodwill has kept us going.

Anna was in deep misery. It seemed to be a combination of many things, mainly loneliness and a need to go 'back home' to Wales. She very rarely cries but she sobs when she tells me. She had very little sleep at Bea's, very little food, and seeing so many loved-ones at such a heightened time upset her, I think. There is also the luxury element of Bea's house, in contrast to the barn.

All these things made me realise how she should have been supervised and supported. It was my job to protect her, and I let her down. I was at home, writing an egotistical piece on a bloody sculpture park; quiet, quiet, writing, when I should have been with her: helping her.

On the evening of Christmas Day I sat down with James and Anna in the kitchen here and tried to tell them how it was for me – how I had let Anna down, how well she had done, how brilliant she is, how I loved them both. How James and I were doing this thing because I believe that when we are together we can do extraordinary things. I spoke and she spoke. The crux of it all was that she wanted to go Home, and Now, Immediately, or very soon after. No more school, no more French, no more France. It was 'a waste of time' being at school, she was not learning anything. She wanted to go back to Wales. I felt shocked, but realised I needed to be clear and strong. I needed to fight for it. I need to come out fighting for it, and make myself fierce for it, even if it pulls up the bottom steel I have.

Mum, Charles and Bea visit us on Boxing Day. The sun shines, we all fit in the one room for a lavish dinner with non-alcohol Champagne. It is great to see Charles, at 6' 4", sitting comfortably by the fire in the red chair. We take them up the track and down to the river. They can see why we love the place. I am so glad the sun is shining.

I took Anna down to the river on Boxing Day and we walked in silence for some time. My stomach was hollow, but I knew we had to talk, so we sat on my mac by the pool in the river and we talked. I told her she was my priority, now. I told her that I would give it my all, that I would pull out all the stops, and if she was still suffering by May, we would look at it again. She was resistant, but listened. She was upset, very upset, and I thought my heart would break for this young girl. But I can't afford it to, there is too much at stake. What we do now will affect us all for the rest of our lives. What we do for Anna will shape how she approaches life in her teenage years and young adulthood.

Anna is a quiet, deep thinker. She is also a lively, talkative girl, so to see her withdrawn in this way has caused great pain to me and to James. I could not sleep. When we spoke, we had to go outside, for privacy. So there have been mornings where we walk up and down the track in the wind, or down by the river. But we have spoken.

We have been through it all, because we now know this cannot continue. We've envisaged separation – I go back to Wales with the kids, he stays here. Repatriation – we all go back and rent a house. These scenarios change day by day. On Monday, for example, I was looking at houses to rent on Anglesey. On Tuesday I thought we might live here forever, after all. James and I still need to talk, the conversation is unfinished, but this Christmas period has brought to light deeper concerns that will resurface, until we resolve them.

I wake. And my stomach is painful, as it is every too-early morning when I wake, with anxiety about Anna. It seems now that when there is trauma it goes deep, to my stomach, not my heart. My father had bowel cancer, and his dad died of the same thing. This comes to me unbidden as I lie there in bed. I need to disperse the core of that hurt, the place it currently resides. To say I am not sure how to do this is neither here nor there, I need to dissipate it, and fast, because I do not want it in me: it needs to go.

It has made me wonder how selfish we are. It has made me realise that I could live like this indefinitely, because it is a better lifestyle for me, after all – digging, writing, thinking, walking, cooking. Cooking slips in there, yes. The time to look after a family: the increasing realisation of the importance of this. The taking on of a role as you put on an apron. The realisation that this is It; you hold the power; you hold the key.

The apron thing is just novelty, but it is a real observation for me, and one I am going to pursue. I need to develop it, for Anna's sake. She needs to see I am in control, that I have no fear. We spoke about fear, or I did, of the language, of the culture. The lead up to Christmas was difficult, with a lack of familiar traditions. What I thought of as little things, like mince pies and carols – Anna missed these. One of the things she mentioned was feeling frightened of the dark, and that if she was lost she would not know whose house to call at.

So I need to be strong, and bold, and attuned to her. We have been together back to Bea's, she and I – Anna navigating on the map, only getting marginally lost and arriving successfully. We have been out together twice, with the emphasis not on shopping, but on meeting family. We drove to the Brocéliande forest to meet up with them all and go for a jungly wood walk. We are together, she and I; we are calm. We have been to McDonald's and she has watched an episode of *Eastenders*, while I studied the roadmap. I am going to investigate a French conversation class this evening.

But I don't know, ultimately, if that is enough. I think and hope it will get easier for her, but I don't know if it will ever be so easy that it becomes a true pleasure and second-nature. I think for the sake of … certainty, surety, ease, they would find school in Wales more enjoyable. It is perhaps the sensible thing to do.

James is patient and kind and loving with Anna. He has changed his mind entirely about how we proceed, having witnessed her deep pain. He has said, we have said, some extraordinary things, in our short walks and intense talks by the river. Perhaps the most profound being his statement that he recognises his 'stubborn principled-ness'. That we would now go back to Wales and rent somewhere, for their sakes. We would remain together, as a family. This is an extraordinary thing, and very new to my heart and ears.

When Anna was explaining why she was unhappy, it was because she did not know the larger scope of language in order to get by with her peers.

'I am learning verbs and colours,' she said, 'but it isn't enough.'

I pointed out how much she has done, has learnt, and how she has made friends, French and English – I mention Tilly.

'She's not a friend,' she said, 'and I think she gets fed-up with having to sit next to me and explain things all the time – *I* would.'

So it's this: this thing. This larger social thing which eventually supercedes everything else. Because Anna is hugely sociable and actively enjoys life. If she was bookish perhaps it would be different, and maybe this is about taking a little of the bookish and adding it in, and taking a little of the ebullience and tempering it. Growing up, in other words. But I would like to give her an environment where she can flourish, and this is what James sees too. She has been 'closed off' as he put it. She misses Wales, much deeper than he thought she would.

And my gardening, and his carpentry, is nothing compared to that. In building a barn, we are trying to make something that lasts longer, that gives them true security, in the long term. We are doing this for ourselves, and for them. Anna at one point in our talk by the river asked me:

'Why are you doing this? This is something only rich people

do. Why didn't you do it when we were younger, or when we are older?'

And she is absolutely right. My responding words about my fear and 'at the time' sound very pale and insubstantial: insignificant. Why didn't we see further, see longer, see it all? Why haven't we got more money, more organisation?

And I tell her she is right – we should have done it when she was younger, or when she is older. Perhaps we will do it when she is older. But we are doing it *now*, for all sorts of reasons, some of which I explain. And it's becoming evident to me that for all the bloody hardship, living in this barn is the right thing to do. Because I have seen parts of all the people in my family I would never otherwise have seen – their beauty and resourcefulness, their frailty and need. I have spent time with them that I would never otherwise have spent. In this particular time, before they change again.

And I tell Anna that if I had only ever done the stuff I was 'supposed' to do, being 'not rich', then I would never have gone to college, or university, or become a designer. We would never have had a house of our own.

The kids go back to school. James and I are recovering from the shock and wondering what happened and how to sift through it all, but there is a sense of normality restored. We do not have the big talk with the children about returning to Wales, but some things remain, must remain for us to see straight and make right decisions, because we must try to avoid the swings and see-saws that come with these traumas.

So, these are the things we are doing. The wind is blowing a gale outside. It is 9.30am and still resolutely grey. Yesterday the sun shone. James and Anna moved the rabbit hutch and I planted out the Christmas tree along the track. Transplanted some foxgloves and imagined the caravan in another aspect, made pretty outside and holidaying our extended family.

These are the things we are doing: Ordering a basketball net.

More books. Writing cards and wrapping presents for the post: January birthdays. Buying more pitta bread from Leader Price. Planning a trip to the beach to find shells for Anna's glue-gun craze. Buying breakfast things and making breakfast a luxury in these dark 6.30am mornings; croissants, pain au choc, thin apple juice. I need to think of her, every step of the way. Making more, rather than less. Being open with James. Talking. And talking more. Focusing on protein (don't forget the hummus, with the pitta).

Tax

French class. A small group of raggle-taggle English folk up above the library: old wallpaper. Homemade jumpers and gap teeth, woolly hats. I follow pronunciation carefully and return home enthused. This enthuses everyone else. '*En deux mille douze j'amerais apprendre le francais.*' '*Nondescript tragedies.*' James knows the sort of people I am trying to describe in my class. There is this strange aura of isolation and loneliness that surrounds these English people. All of a certain age, still struggling after five years of being here. They seem quite kind and nice, but sad somehow. Their pronunciation is awful, French spoken in an English accent. So much so that I cringe, and feel complacent that my accent is not so bad – this offsets my appreciation that they know far more vocabulary than I do. I realise it is all about confidence, about belief in how you communicate the words. The teacher's words are succinct and beautiful, I enjoy hearing how she moves from the *h* to the *ll*, the rounded endings.

Drive to St Jean Brévelay to discover the *pépinière*. Rush to accomplish this new mission. Feel unfurling, an opening out: *I can do this.*

I don't trust it but it would be so lovely if it lasts. French no longer alien perhaps, the roads no longer so unfamiliar. French something I can do – it opens out, keeps opening out, without fear. *Pépinière* is shut. Drive home and am now facing the kitchen.

Later, I find the other *pépinière*, which is somebody's house with a few overpriced rhododendrons in the garden. Nice people, and an accomplishment to find it. Anna and I continue our drive over to Guénin and the ancient church. Guénin dead as a doornail at 3pm on a Saturday afternoon. We buy a baguette and carry on to Baud pool.

The water is high, swill and inviting, filled with humidity and echo. It is a round, friendly pool. There are a lot of ladies standing in the reception area and no-one rushes to serve us; a plateau before classes finish and the public is let in.

When we get back to the barn I order myself a *Miss Mary from Sweden* swimdress online, with a view to joining Anna in the pool. This will save me wearing Bea's old cossie, which is becoming a bit threadbare around the arse. I am 42 after all, I tell myself.

In the evening I dig my 'burial ground' as Joe calls my *barriere*, when he comes out into the beautiful evening. It is still, with a pink sky. We go for a walk up the track, the moon is full in the east, the sun set in the west. We've talked about the book he will write and I attempt hopeless plots. He is interested in the sacrificial site at Guénin, it could be 'inspiration'. We see some boys on bikes with the big blonde dog running behind them. They skid to dusty halts and watch us walk our way back down the track to the barn as the light goes.

Sunday. Went for a walk around Guénin hill. God, but it was boring. I picked up some pinecones. Anna had a face on her like murder, but I kept on thinking: *at least she's not in Matalan, at least she's not in Matalan.* A mantra, as I swung my arms with those pine cones.

It is stange how a day can be brim full of extremes – from one to the other. It has been like that recently. This morning I had terrible palpitations, which laid me out on the landing and back to bed. Hyperventilating, quite scary, for over an hour. James helped me, staying with me and telling me how to breathe. Trying to focus the breath away from my heart, down to my stomach. Slow, then, drive into Pontivy *SuperU* and NOZ for a quick camelia fix. Home now, dinner on the go. Anna blithe. She got great results in her Maths test.

On the drive to the bus this morning, Joe sings while Anna practices naming Parts of the Body and Colours. Joe did some verb conjugation around 7am. They have language tests today. I didn't get much sleep, feel like I am staggering through the days. Staggering or limping, I'm not sure.

I take a break from the computer and walk up the track. There's a heavy dew, but otherwise dry and still. I come out of the big barn door straight onto Mr Rufus, who looks cold and hungry in his hutch. There is birdsong and a pale-blue mist. The field grass is that in-between green. It has a sheen of moisture and stands still. I walk up the track wondering about French tax systems and The Meaning Of It All.

Walking back down the track towards the barn I look at the blue chimney smoke, rising in a straight line from the reddish roof. It is the cover of *Little Grey Rabbit and the Wandering Hedgehog,* a tiny dog-eared book that has followed me around my whole life. A rustic idyll. Most people spend their whole working lives dreaming of such a situation, such a lifestyle, and we are living it. I'm selling articles, I've got more work on the horizon, and am even thinking of making some small paintings. Creative things. The next question that James and I touched upon during last night's evening walk, was, 'Is it sustainable?'

There is Anna's wellbeing. She is fine now, but we have to think of the longterm. Then there is his business. Now that we are in the loop, with the SIRET (business registration) number, we begin to receive mail that pulls us further in, requesting money. *Taxe Foncière* – the French equivalent of Council Tax. I suggest we get the accountant to help us fill in that form. As we are living quite ad hoc, it seems bizarre to pay for this particular barn-living arrangement as though it were a regular house.

'What would you call it?' I ask, for the purpose of filling in these forms.

I have been thinking about Dreams – about trying to achieve the Ideal in life. My initial dream on meeting James – rural idyll, animals – trying to recreate the childhood scene perhaps, before it all went pear-shaped. And the decimation of dreams – it is actually quite liberating. Or maybe it is now that the dream has been realised, if only to an extent, the dream can be set free. One no longer has to *strive* for it. I am weighing up practicalities, trying to be objective.

I found great freedom yesterday in the idea of Giving Up. Giving In. Accepting the inevitable, what Is – certainly where money and property are concerned. Who do I think I am? As Anna said, after all, it is rich people who do what we are doing. Sure enough big houses usually have big wages accompanying them.

My friend, Patrick, emails. *How do you find it?*

Expensive.

I find other things – the cultural things – a boy kissing his father, cheek to cheek, before he gets out of the van and goes to school. This kissing, that contact, you don't see or receive in the UK. Those things then, that make me think of all these churches, in every square in every village and town. Religious education is not taught at school, but I suspect all these churches are well-attended. In which case that would make France a more religious country than Britain. I think that shows. They have much less of the Americanised shit that permeates British culture. At least, none that I have seen – they have advertising and marketing, but it seems somehow less pervasive, more naïve. That may just be my reading of it, as it's a foreign language and we are out in the sticks, after all.

I go for lunch and conversation with Rebecca in her Tahitian-inspired house. Textiles and colour, candles and crockery. A visual balm. Talked about painting, books, all sorts of diverting things. I don't know that these ideas would ever produce a proper income – cash, maybe. On leaving, I follow her down the track, her little red Peugeot kicking up dust before me. We pull over; she points out the route to the *pépinière* and zooms off.

I am in the middle of practically nowhere with no *pépinière* in sight. I pass a fat man putting up a sign on the corner: 'Maisie's Café – Fish & Chips.' I stop, put on the hazard lights.

'Excuse me, do you know of a garden centre, nursery, near here?'

'No, love, not round here. There's two on the way to *SuperU*, I think.'

Ah, bollocks, I think – *Rebecca has sent me on a wild goose chase… but she sounded so sure…*

I drive a little further, and there it is, the upside-down sign, just as she said it would be, leading further inland to a *proper garden centre*. Praise be. I check it out briefly then drive on in time to meet the school bus. I grab a solitary *éclair* and recover/contemplate today's intense three-hour conversation. I think about tonight's French class. I pick up the kids and drive home. In my class, they don't know the word *pépinière*. They have lived here for seven years… They *do* know past tense verb conjugations though, which I do not. I continue to find the French teacher's voice lovely.

I talk to James, post-class, about an objective approach to problem-solving. I explain my simple 'admit defeat' approach, which encompasses the idea of not struggling to borrow money and pay it back. He had spent the day with a couple of builders, with their various stories of ending up in court over tax errors, and paying 1,000 euros a month in insurances alone. He has met other tradesmen – English blokes, usually married to French women – who are making it work. The figures they quote for insurance alone is horrifying – the figures are very obviously beyond our means. It is expensive here. I find it with food, though other people don't, so maybe I am missing something. I find ordering English books through Amazon racks up. Food, petrol, school dinners and transport.

I'm sitting at the kitchen table. It is still early morning and the sky is that baby pink and blue, as pale as the iced field. The world is frozen. All that 'bleak midwinter' stuff that should have been here at Xmas has arrived now. It is hard cold, glittering cold, with stars and moon very much still up as I scrape the ice off the car and take the kids to school. I do not intend to go anywhere today. Staying still is the only way of not spending money. I hang some big white sheets on the line – white against white sky and white earth.

It has been a week of almost continuous talking. We have looked at it from most every angle. I have thought of listing the various scenarios:

Scenario 1: We build a business here and pay all the associated French contributions.

Scenario 2: We go back to Wales and rent somewhere.

There have been many more, including 'signing on' but the conclusion seems to have been reached through a process of elimination. One circular part of this thinking was that in order to earn the 48,000 euros a year needed to survive in this system, James would have to work full-out, full-throttle, full-time for his clients. Which he could do, but it would leave absolutely no time, and no money, for barn renovation. We are beginning to pay Business Rates, Council Tax (French style), Income Tax, Social Security contributions. In short, when it comes to the brink, this point we are now at, James acknowledges that he does not want to be part of this 'oppressive' tax regime, on a never-ending wheel of efficient working, in order simply to stay within the system.

We discuss at length and seem to be reaching a decision to return home. This is a massive change on James's part, from a point of view that has been embedded in a pro-French lifestyle for the past five years, so it will take me a little while to get used to the idea. Not that long, but a little while. This is partly why I expect the decision to change again. I think this especially when he gets a request for a quote on a big job. A job that would see us through a good six months. Then, my mind switches once more:

Maybe we can make it work, stay here, I think.

The options flow in and out of my mind almost seamlessly now, as I move earth to my planting ground, my *barriere*. It is a sunny Sunday; Joe sits whittling a spoon and everything shines with light and colour. Another walk along the river where James reiterates the decision.

'No, that email did not change my mind, I do not want to enter the French system.'

So we discuss moving back to Wales – how, when. How. When. He thinks more immediately than I do. We discuss broad overview and detail. Some of the detail can wait, but such changes inevitably make the mind run on, and I begin to browse rentals online, at night when I can't sleep.

'We could live in a static caravan,' James suggests. 'It would be cheaper.'

'*No!*' I am horrified. 'I'm not living in a bloody static caravan – that's part of the problem, that Anna has nowhere really to go in the house, no real living space.'

So I look at £650+ houses online and there they are, in outback Anglesey, with an outbuilding. So I play that lifestyle in my head, quickety quick, and am left cold.

Later I am sitting waiting for the kids at the bus-stop, alone in the car with the infinitely grey day hanging around outside. I am looking at the ornate buildings around the church square and thinking about Welsh towns and house prices. And I think, actually, James is right. If we do go back to Wales, then *we rent the cheapest thing we can find*. If it is a caravan, or a tipi, so much the better. The purpose of returning is for the kids to go to school, to be happy with their friends. What I do not want to do is to make a return to our former situation, with the relentless cycle of earning and spending. With the imbalance and not least the *time* I spend working – out of the house all day with barely a 'good morning', and always too tired for conversation or play in the evening.

Getting something cheap would alleviate all that. It would

mean I would not have to work full-time – perhaps I could continue with a freelance lifestyle, even. Or, if I did go back to full-time work, part of the wage could be saved up, so that we could fund building the barn with it. A long shot, a tall order, but a feasible route perhaps.

I think to myself, we would need to keep costs *down*, in order to make the long term benefits. This would mean:

- No internet.
- No phone.
- No TV.

Ideally no bloody Council Tax and Water Rates. And low fuel bills. It is difficult to live in Britain like that, with all the system wanting More, and Everything, but it is only a perception, my perception, that makes this so. *Here*, we pay nothing for where we live – fuel is free, house is free, and it has given me a real freedom, to think. *There*, I feel I would be straight back into the flat spin of work/rent/work, with no benefit to show for it. The benefit would be for the kids, of course. For them to have the security and pleasure of their friends about them, to know the language and terrain, the confidence that gives.

A lot of what James and I talk about is the need not to repeat the mistakes we have made in the past. This is to do with money, where we live, how we balance the responsibilities of working life and family between us. That is my greatest concern, because from my point of view, I am walking back into exactly the same thing I have just walked away from. He tells me it will be different this time, our living in Wales together. I listen and I believe him.

We have to inform all the French authorities that we are moving back. It will take time, I think, to do this properly: to pull out.

'I don't want to jump,' I say.

James's birthday. I intend to make King Tiger Prawn curry, but

I'm not entirely sure how, and I suspect I need to be *confident* to pull it off. Are *crevettes* the same as prawns?

In these few days, I've been getting used to bracing myself before opening the door. Actually, cold air is okay, as long as you're prepared for it.

The decision we've made – to return to Wales – keeps washing over me. It is a dawning realisation. We still haven't told the kids – James will take the lead in that. The time has not yet been right, I suspect because we are still absorbing it ourselves.

A long time ago I must have read a story about a secret garden. Not the rather dry book by Frances Hodgson Burnett, but one that gave me the mental image of dark green undergrowth under a large square window. Within this garden was a deep pool, with the flash of orange fish. Secret, darkest green. Much of the time I'm outside shifting soil is spent in a sort of daydream, a visioning of this green. Of rhododendrons, growing so large they form a forest. This is how I envisage the barn if we have to leave it dormant for a long patch of time. All the weeds will grow back, when I determined that would never be. We could get a gardener to come and mow the grass and keep on top of the weeds, but I know that will never happen. Every time we come here the first three weeks will be spent trying to tame once more that which has been left to grow untamed. Maybe. I hope of course that it is not dormant for too long, but perhaps it will be, and perhaps it has to be this way.

The knowledge we will definitely be leaving sets a certain sense of pace to what I now do. I buy plastic boxes and sift through all our stuff from the attic, organising it so that all is neat and accounted for. I plant those rhododendrons. I think about spraying weed-killer in the hope that somehow I will mutate into one of those English people that Know What They're Doing and is Efficient. None of these people are how you think they are going to be. I saw Tilly's mum yesterday, a woman who I had imagined must be devilishly proactive and practical. The sort of woman who has a Hoovered boot to her car and provides Healthy Snacks. Terrifying. Of course she looks a perfectly nice, ordinary, understated woman.

There is still a vestigial anxiety left in me that James will change his mind, that the goalposts will change again. We have discussed so much, I guess it is natural to be tired now. We have thought of the end of the school year as a time to move and we are agreed on this. I don't think James will change his mind now, but we will need to talk more.

One thing I need to be careful of is that I respond very quickly to things. I get excited and see certain things – like this new potential work of James's – as Answering All Our Needs, providing the one magic thing that will tip the balance in our glorious favour. It doesn't work like that. It is a dogged and persevering, attention-to-financial-detail approach that may see us through to the end. The constant goal is to not plummet into a financial whirpool. I feel optimistic.

Going back to lecturing work has its own set of challenges. I need to avoid falling into old-time habits – the self-deprecation, the overstimulus, the dull body and lazy mind, working like a machine. I don't believe in it anymore; the poky office, the petty politics. I think that, through all this, James has come around to some of my way of thinking, and I have come around to some of his.

There are bursts of birds by the roadside, flocks of starlings as I drive past; they turn in the light alongside. Cattle in misty fields, picturesque church spires, as though to say, *Ah, so this is the authentic French Scene.*

A buzzard, on my right, rising as I drive from the *pépinière* in Keraudren, the place where there is only one road. Just now, the birds rise up and flow in unison, across the window as I walk to the sink. They fly to the bare branches of the oak tree, pale tawny on brown, and settle so that you would never know they were there. There is a pheasant, plump under the oak tree in the gloom; a thrush, blackbird, robin – I don't know all their names, but they must be here now the ground has thawed. We need to buy them yet more seed.

I wonder if this is how it might be – just an appreciation of this place for what it is, rather than a psychological striving for what it might be. I think of those plants, again. Think of how it might be in the gentle spring sun, with all those birds and greenery.

In the space of half an hour, I manage to fuck up several things.

The *Miss Mary skirted swimsuit* I ordered at great expense, posted to the UK and then on to France, was MASSIVEGINORMOUS – not even worth trying on. Back it goes, in the hope that they redeem my dosh in the fourteen day limit…

Then, in the midst of clearing up James's birthday wrapping paper, I manage to put the VAT payment document in the fire. In the fucking fire. I don't remember doing it, but I must have done. I look through both bins, twice, and come out smelling of bananas and teabags, but no document. Next I accidentally trap Joe's hands in the big back door, as he is hanging off the roof trying to get the basketball. Bloody hell. I explain to the kids I am taking myself off on a solitary walk, out of the way of further damage. They nod sagely.

James is ill. It is grey and I feel flat, but better now after a trip to the shop, to see that there are people out there, surviving, and that I can communicate a little. I will go to my class tonight as well. I will make chicken curry before I go. I fantasise about Greek sunshine, clean spacious rooms with cleaners, fresh white linen and warm gentle breezes.

Quiet, so quiet. Fire lit. I spend the morning with my magic apron on; cleaning, washing sheets, hanging them in the still grey air. It was so knuckle-gnawingly boring yesterday that on our Sunday river walk Joe and I decided to go to the McDonalds in Locminé. He wolfed a burger and I looked at the French property paper. It got me thinking. I need to be mindful of over-optimism, of the idea that everything is going to be fine 'later'

– that I am going to magically inherit some vast amount, or sell a blockbuster. Is there a way to buck the system, or is working life until retirement 'it'?

Living quietly like this makes me think of how it will be when we are old; heat and food the main daily concerns. It makes me think of Nana and Eb and how they lived, of Granny and Grandpa, and how they live. How we all end up, with our few sticks of bits that form a home: familiar. Enough to get by and live quietly, without financial stress. Is that the best we can hope for? Do we build this house and leave it for the children? How do we see out our ancient years? It feels like this still period is a natural time for quiet reflection. I feel certain this is what it is intended for, before I have to dive into the rush again, if I do. I'm weighing up what renting means, what working means, what poverty and 'managing' mean.

I read in the paper of an unemployed man in Liverpool who lives on much less than £67 a week – it gave a list of all the things he paid for in that sum. He lives on 25p rice and pasta from Tesco. On the opposite page it had a short piece about the proposed 'Royal yacht'. How many billions of pounds there? The yacht will be maintained, in part, by university students staying there on science trips. Right.

My magic apron is now pulling me back towards the sink. Career women everywhere – if having domestic identity crisis, wear a stiff linen apron. Strange transformation, honest.

It is 'hypnotism', James reckons. Same if you put on a business suit, or a uniform, perhaps.

It's 4pm. I am cooking Welsh Cakes on the stove, using pieces of fallen oak to fuel it. Far out.

I am thinking back to the reason we bought the barn. I don't know how to work out the balance of doing it up, yet not living here. I don't know how, or if, it adds up. The recent experience of shelling out lots of money on travel backwards and forwards is still with me. I suppose what I know now is that we will not live here permanently, with all that entails; with children in school and us earning a living. Perhaps we will live here, James and I, at some later date. Perhaps it will be a 'retreat'.

We spent an hour thinking about whether he/we could do that big job, talking through the quote. Someone else's renovation project, the image of their house sitting on the screen while we discuss all the ramifications the job would entail. The details now include factoring in a Welsh workshop, travel, working on site and the wheel of working on other people's houses. If only there was a way we could afford to have James work solely on the barn, I continue to muse. I don't know what that way is. Ideally and imaginatively, I can see it, but when it comes down to the realities and expense of living, I just don't see how.

I do some work, then sort a tiny bit of the attic in my new plastic boxes. Now I will go out and buy a few bits before picking up the kids. This afternoon I will go with Anna to Leclerc and do a big shop. It feels like hard work, the sky is determinedly sullen, but I feel that somehow, against the odds, we might get somewhere with it all. If James has a few straight weeks on the barn, I think we would see visible developments. That is not too far-fetched.

Enthusiasm.

This morning, drove early to the school bus as usual. Dropped off the kids and picked up a baguette; the neon lights pink against the *boulangerie* wall, a pastry magnet in the dark. It would look good in a film. Took 100 euros out of the bank. Drove back, gave James a *pain au raisin* and received five soft kisses. Yummy. He is off to work; I am off to the *pépinière*, with the map and a magnifying glass to read it. Got mildly lost but made it, and there are all the plants, just waiting to be looked at. All open, and my poor French just enough to get by with the owner, who leaves me to it. I spend a lovely time looking through the polytunnels and eventually choose two big rhodos, a rosemary and something else, I don't know what, with pale greeny grey leaves that I like. I come back, I shovel down two *pain au chocolat* and some tea while standing up at the kitchen window. It is sunny and I dig and plant and sit on the steps I made in the sun. It makes perfect sense.

I think, I will make Wales where I have to be for work-life, and here I will invest all my love and energy for soul-life. There will be a crossover, but that seems a good plan. James and I will come here *together*, and work on it *together*. And, over time, it may increase in financial value, but the value to us nevertheless will be that it is *ours*.

I plant with enthusiasm. I don't know whether it is the planting which gives me enthusiasm, but I know it is good for me. This morning the birds were singing, and that is what this place has – peace and beauty. In spades. So my language is limited, yes, but it is a lot better than it used to be, and good enough that I can make myself understood. I need to learn more and I will. How great to see something manifest that I have thought about for so long, though. The rhodos are just the right height to form a proper immediate screen. I have planted two. I am going to go back and buy MORE.

I am going to buy:

A conifer.

A lilac.

Four more rhodos. I could make that eight. I hope they live.

Yesterday I bought pansies and these have gone into a blue pot and a small red pot. I picked up the red pot at the *Intermarché* when I had to return last night to get the right cereal for Joe. It was cheap (the pot, not the cereal). It sits on the white table. The blue pot sits on the wooden table on the concrete patio. I planted the small heather, rosemary and the un-named thing in the 'kitchen garden'.

Again. *Encore*. French class last night a reminder of how beautiful the language sounds, coming out of Maryvonne's patient self, and how ghastly it sounds in an English accent, by rote, with no intonation. Today, this morning, again. 100 euros out the bank, fill up the car with petrol. Tell no-one, as might be forming a habit more expensive than crack cocaine. Drive across country, nonchalantly putting the roadmap under the seat. I know the way. I know what to do, in terms of arranging the seats so that everything fits.

I drive past the lake. Frost this morning: baby-blue skies and pink washes. The road curves hard past the water, just becoming light. Mist furling up, individual spirals forming a wraithlike landscape. A heron banks to my right, broad wings diagonal, grey against grey, pewter and silver nitrate.

I enjoy this route across country seeing the different trees and shrubs. There are austere houses with *Chartreuse* shutters, weatherbeaten blue paintwork on more ramshackle cottages, a goat in the garden. How fabulous formal, manicured green shrubs look against old stonework.

The guy at the nursery must think his boat has come in. I pile up the evergreens and struggle through some inadequate French. He labours over the transaction, and still there is no deduction for hard cash. Shame. So here I am, back home with a coffee and baguette, standing up, looking out the window planning where I will plant.

Heron

I am trying to scoop out some magic formula that almost exists in my thinking soup – I nearly have it but it continues to turn over on itself. The formula needs to go something like:

James + barn = house.

There is money involved, the borrowing of money, which immediately means money going *out*, so it does not add up at the moment. It also means a presumption that James has the motivation to work on the barn, which he has said he does not. Again we discussed selling it. We decide not to, at least not for now.

We talked about approaching it from a 'business-like' angle, but this presupposes that we would do it up with the motivating force being to sell it, for profit, within a set timeframe.

I have always thought that James's work would add value to this house, over and above what we paid for it. If we borrowed £10,000 to do the floors and roof, that would increase the overall value far greater than that sum. If this barn is currently worth E80,000 (*if* it is) and we borrowed £50,000 over two years, we would have spent £130,000 on it. Would it be worth any more than that? Possibly. Possibly not. But that would require James working on it continuously, away from us, which we no longer want to do.

It is damn cold. 8.25am. It is still dark, just gradually lightening. To heat our entire pod-home we burn wood that is largely offcuts of floorboards and doors from James's jobs – we spend no money on fuel. I wonder whether living like this is an artform in itself.

What we have to do now is distentangle ourselves from the French social security and tax system. There is one word I would remind myself of, if ever I look back regretfully and think, *Aw, we should have tried harder*. It is this: *Cotisations*. Nightmare. Don't let anyone tell you otherwise. We received a bill in the post for 6,000 euros, payable in three instalments. This is the French equivalent of National Insurance, apparently. It is The Big One, but alongside that you're required to have *decennales* (public liability insurance) and a *mutuelle*, to cover the 30% health insurance that the *cotisation* doesn't cover. I remember reading all this stuff in the Living and Working in France books, after the initial rush of buying the barn, and dimly recall it not adding up at the time. It was an amber warning light even then, but you can't live your life by books, can you? I seem to have to experience it for myself, before I learn.

We are doing all this after the trend, of course. By now, most Artisans have realised it just doesn't add up, and they've all gone back to the UK, or are in the process of going. Today I look online at prices of *longères* – the part-renovated ones, the renovated ones, and the wrecks. The difference between French and English prices remains, with a 3-bed detached house, fully renovated with land available here for around 100,000 euros. By our reckoning the barn might fetch 75,000. But the website is full of these properties – 'Price Reduction!' in red on each one. It is an indicator.

The photos tell their own stories. A surprising amount are renovated in the same sort of way – woodburning stove, fitted kitchen, colour tiles. Then there are the photos which show the part-renovation. Pictures of plasterboard and fiberglass and halfmade walls, next to tumble driers, fridges and shower-rooms, the towels flung over the side of the bath. Over the empty kitchen tables-with-matching-sets-of-chairs, in largely empty rooms, you can imagine the conversations that result in the decision to sell. All those stories, all those shattered dreams. If we had moved here five years ago, some of these pictures might be ours – a family that had tried it and had now given up, given in, or simply moved on.

James has used the word 'failure' several times, and I think he probably feels it far more deeply than he lets on. The only saving grace is that we don't owe banks huge amounts of money. We talk again: *We sell the barn/we keep the barn.* She loves me, she loves me not.

Given the stress of selling, and the feeble amount we would get for it, plus having to submerge ourselves in a giant mortgage again if we buy in the UK, we discuss keeping the barn.

'To what end?' questions James.

'As an expression of ourselves.' As something that exists, that we have actively sought. Something we are involved with, on a psychological and physical level. In the main, now, and later sporadically, perhaps. To see whether we can renovate it, piece by piece, year on year, to a place which has a different function to the one we have been thinking about for the past five years. It does not have to be a family home, with workshop. It can be simply two large rooms, for sitting in and contemplation. The main thing is that it has to be structurally sound. It needs foundations, a new roof, a floor, walls, windows and doors.

So this decision-making process is the underlying thread to our current everyday work. It is bitterly cold, the north wind whips through your bones. I found an old sheepskin coat in the caravan and went out for a late afternoon walk. With my fur snood on, I looked, finally, like a tramp. I couldn't move my arms much, and smelt of caravan, but I was warm.

I am happy. Why am I happy? I walk along the river dressed like *Sir Digby Chicken Caesar.* The great thing about this coat is you can take it off and lie in the sun, in the blisteringly cold air, and get a tan.

I am happy because last night James and I discussed the seven root delusions of Buddhism. We talked about Karma, what it is, and how we own it. He explained a lot to me, and I intuit he should study Divinity. Then I realise he already is.

He says that all the religions – Hinduism, Tao, Christianity, all say the same thing.

In response to what I ask about 'attachment', he says that the things we have as possessions – cars, tables, chairs, are not really possessions, that they can be taken away from us at any time. The real possessions are what we speak – what we say, our deeds. It is a new and revolutionary thought to me. He talks about organised religion, and how it is not true religion, but a form of control. He says that nirvana is not 'some other place' – God does not sit on a cloud, but is truly within us.

It is very complicated and very simple at the same time. It has shown me that there might be a way for me to get over the sticking points I find in life. I feel perhaps that the second root delusion – 'Anger' – is something I am going to examine in myself and meditate on. Anger and Money are two themes I need to look at. They are interlinked, I think, manifesting themselves in slightly poisonous thoughts. I find it fascinating.

I am happy because I see in him a strong thread which we are sharing. It may be something we can develop and continue to share. I am happy because I have finished Raj's book. It is being printed and is on its way to me. I am happy because perhaps there is a meaningful future for the barn as a home for our energies. I am happy because it is sunny, because it is freezing cold, because I put seeds out for the birds, and because the children are so resilient.

At French class last night, the lady with the poor pronunication knew the names of all the birds in the garden. It is quite soporific, sitting there listening to them talk about chaffinches, robins and buzzards, pointing out the pictures in Maryvonne's book. Our homework is a page of *bricolage/jardinière* tools which we have to name and sort.

Maryvonne has brought in a piece of sweetcorn kernel which

is excellent for cleaning shovels. I have never even *considered* cleaning a shovel. Shovels, after all, are just shovels. When we are describing what we have done this week I explain I have been mostly sitting by the fire. It is the coldest winter in Europe for fourteen years. I am aware how slow my French is. We talk about the severe weather. I ask her what she has done this week. Not much, she says. She has made seedcakes for the birds and then sat in her chair and watched them eat it. She has varnished the birdbox with linseed oil.

I have this vision of this organised and pleasant woman, with her organised and pleasant life, sitting in a warm conservatory identifying birds. She is trim and relaxed, eternally patient with us. I wonder what it is like to be like that. I wish I was. She would not dream of moving abroad, harum-scarum, but had a longstanding job in her community before retiring and doing this part-time evening work. She knows all the people, all the places. She is calm and enjoys life. Everything has its place. How lovely to be like that. The class is unhurried, challenging but not excitable. I think how different that is from my teaching style.

This morning on the kitchen table is the glossy pamphlet Joe brought back from school. They had a careers day, where they select options – Architect, Policeman, Lawyer, Plumber etc. Joe was interested in architecture, but there were too many people selecting that, so for his second choice 'the Professions' came into play: Carpenter. The big glossy leaflet is promotional material for a big builder in the area – presumably one who provides apprenticeships. The other leaflets are government ones sporting lots of pie-charts. The leaflet made it clear to me and James that we do not want to encourage Joe in a building trade (in fact, it really isn't his style. International Finance would be more likely). But I explained to James this morning that I think it important that Joe help him with some form of building/construction/labour, so Joe gets his own 'Apprenticeship' at home.

This evening I meet a neighbour up the track who I've not spoken to before. We have a chat. Snow due. Difficult to explain that I know I look ridiculous in my dodgy sheepskin coat, but I think he understood.

The sound of blowtorch on the frozen pipes, in the dark early morning. Plumes of steam around the sink at the kitchen window, to defrost Mr Rufus's drinking water.

After school run and computer work I sit outside and contemplate sun and cold air.

Later I take Joe and A to buy new sportshoes. I tell James he doesn't need to come, that I am 'psychologically prepared' for the sports shop. But I'm not. Both Joe and Anna want to be out of there as soon as possible, and every *soldes* boot I show meets with a groan of disapproval. Joe selects two pairs to try on. I say, 'as long as they fit and you like them, I don't care how much they cost.' *Mistake.* This is a Mistake, because the shoes that fit him and that he likes are 75E.

So, I have managed to spend 135E in the past two days, and I have no money coming into my account. I find the whole experience of the synthetically laden Sports 2000 shop depressing – mainly because I have just hammered my card, and can't believe I could be so stupid. Why didn't I *engage* more? How could I have engaged more? I could have taken stock; I could have said, 'Yes, Joe, they are nice, but can you please find something cheaper?'

I should have been properly Mentally Prepared. It depresses me utterly, overpriced *le coq sportif* deck shoes made in Indonesia, sold to this mug of an Englishwoman. My lack of language. Feeling proud that I managed to say the previous size was 'too small' for him, really just isn't enough. But mainly it is these two things: that children and living cost money, and that I am going to have to return to a nine-to-five job to afford the things that life and children need. It doesn't seem to matter, in the event, whether you own a house or not, you still need an income to pay for stuff. If you do have a mortgage or need to pay rent, it just means more of your income is disposed of in this way.

The shoes experience made me think that this is sheer fantasy, a thoroughly foolish notion; the idea of renovation, of continuing to maintain this place. How? With what money?

Then after feeling quite blue, I tried to get a handle on my 'negative doubting' and thought, *What if we are right, though? What if we have got it right? What if it is the right idea*? And I try to live in the now and enjoy the moment. Enjoy the sunlight, the air and reading the plant book. Sometimes the plants I've planted seem to glow with what they might one day be, and sometimes they look like leggy rhododendrons that have reached their full height, thin and never tall enough.

It is bizarre. I can't sleep at night, the moon is full. I make up my mind that it is financially ridiculous to keep the barn. Every penny we earn we will need just to get by. I explain all that to James, and we are agreed.

'It is abstract to me anyway,' he says.

We draw a line under it. If I had seen Susan at the school bus I would have told her our intentions and invited her round to value the place. As it is, I do it myself, online. We would be looking at around 50,000 euros, I reckon. James thinks 40. The internet is full of renovations and derelicts, some with better roofs than this for less money. But I was adamant yesterday, and this morning when I wake up it is still clear as day. We sell.

I speak to my mum on the phone. I am standing on the track with my fingers freezing around my mobile, I look back at the barn as I talk to her in the sunshine. The smoke coming from the chimney is whipped away on the cold wind. I look at the soft-red tile roof, feel how it will look when the caravan is gone, exposing the length of the building and new grass growth.

Ahh, I think.

How can I put it on one of those internet sites, to be pored over and compared with others in the stark light of day? Isn't this barn a bit *different* to all the other wrecks? I feel compassion towards it, the opposite of all the financial rationale I have just carried out!

How can I think something so decisively one day, and think another thing the very next? When the satellite man was here, he said his compass couldn't work out what was going on with this place, it couldn't tell north from west: it kept spinning around. Maybe the compass of the mind has a similar reaction. I think we are on a funny line here. Maybe the quartz has something to do with that.

Yesterday afternoon, when I was fully resigned to never spending any money, ever again; horrified at the eternal spiralling of my overdraft, disillusioned and disappointed – when I realised I could not justify expenditure on wisteria, that possibly I never could – I got an email asking if I'd be interested in some work, commissioning me to the tune of £4,500. It couldn't be more opportune.

At the time I am so knackered and brain-fried that I just say 'yeah'. I am not hullabaloo and I do not think that money will solve everything, but it takes the sting out of the next couple of months. The travel back to Britain and fierce rent. James is working to earn money for us to make the return journey and to afford living costs in Wales, but this work will help.

The sun is bright and I sit in it even though the wind is cold, in my sheepskin. I accept the fact that I see this place in a romantic light. I see its potential realised, visually, in my mind's eye – the wooden windows, set in golden stone. Even if it does not all add up. What a strange thing it all is. It is like love can be – idealising, idolising.

But what of the Buddhist theory of removing Illusions and *seeing things as they are*? That is what I was trying to do in looking at finances; recognising, identifying and putting a stop to the continual slipping into decline. That is what I was trying to do with the Buddhist idea of removing Attachments – dis-attaching ourselves, by selling the barn. Trying to see things for what they are, not what I would like them to be. I was thinking of the *Running with the Wolves* book, of how she talks about *knowing when to let go*.

I had decided that we may not like selling the barn, but financially it was the sensible thing to do. And then today, I changed my mind.

Epiphany. It is so fragile, this feeling, so clear.

Don't sell. Keep. Enjoy. Must be the sun. I am aware I am the granddaughter of a small-town bank manager, which must have left traces. I am aware I am the daughter of a creative rainbow mother, who gave money to strangers on the train. Out of all this, I am conscious of money and creativity. But I know, with an unshakeable certainty today, that we should not sell, that we should try to find a way to build it, over time. As Emma said about her Shetland island hut, 'It is more valuable to us than what it is worth.' Or something. Lots and lots of somethings.

I think to myself: Keep Kersparlec. Do what we can. Love. Eat. Look after the children and each other. Work, but not harder than we need to. Minimise effort. It might not take *that* much to make part of the barn look ok. I must do the work that is in front of me, and all the other things, with good grace and the belief that it will all be fine.

Drove the car onto a concrete ramp outside the shop. In the shape of an instant, the day changes from, 'Ok, just bought a bathmat from GiFi,' to a state of emergency balls-up. Car stuck on ramp. Can't go forward, can't go back. Like a turtle on its back, scraping metal. Concerned women with babies stop to try and help. I can only wonder WTF. Find myself standing outside the car, hands on hips, thinking, *What would a man do?* Steered off the ramp to the right and it worked.

The fields have been spread with muck – pigshit taken by the farmer from our very own resident pigshed factory – so the land is thick with the smell of ammonia. So bad I don't want to go out in it. I walk along the Blavet with Joe and a lot of chocolate. I feel rubbish.

James is very quiet. He says he wants to turn his back on the barn. For a while I feel angry at this. And then later I see he is right, that I need to let go. I have not been very good at this in the past, tending to cling on, to wait until the thing is down around my knees. You could view this as tenacious, dogmatic or determined, and any of these might be true. Fact is, it is difficult to let go of your dreams.

So I have to acknowledge the full extent of *experiencing* the dream, such as it has been, these long five years or so – complicated, difficult and in places fantastic. We tried to make our dream a reality, and to some extent it worked. Not the full extent; we go back out there older and less naïve where money and buying property are concerned – at least I hope so.

I feel demoralised and exhausted. I wait for my batteries to recharge by lying under a red blanket, willing some of the rich-colour energy into me. Anna and James are reading a French homework book, and Joe is trying to make sense of his. Anna's school trip to the Opera resulted in a lot of pictures on Facebook, and it is immensely calming and gratifying to see her photograph folder of *amis*. That is the success. The rest is just money and taxes.

Out of the corner angle of the kitchen window, a chance view of seagulls flocking over the edge of the wide field, bright white wings against brown shit and straw, dull grey clouds. It is the view I loved seeing as I drove about in Wales, and here it is, right on my doorstep, made immediate. We see it again as we drive up the road, careful in the car as the clutch is about to go. Joe points out the tractor and the gulls gathering behind, picking up all the seeds as he puts them down.

I'm getting over this general *malaise*. I sit on a step in the sun and fall in love with it all over again. I repeat James's line: 'turning my back on it', to harden and recommit myself to the idea. But the rhodos look so pretty in the sun. I sit out there for a long time, drink tea and listen to Anna singing. She and Joe do their French reading with James – he is eternally patient, for hours and hours. He makes good food and we walk by the river before it gets dark or rains.

We let the children know we will return to Wales. There is no great drama, just gentle acceptance, over dinner. We tell Michel, Thérèse and Ange. They are surprised, but understanding.

I look online for cheap houses and land for sale in Wales. Those houses that would have been £40K ten years ago now have that extra £100K on top.

Two herons stand every morning in the sage-green field outside the one and only kitchen window. They face south, the same way but with some distance between them. Stock-still, tall like storks. They are sunbathing, I think. When they get disturbed they rise, unhurried, and wheel back to the lake. I wear a peg in my hair and hang out the laundry.

'Here, look at this,' James says, taking a piece of paper from his back pocket.

Constant Brillant, it reads. It is the handmade business card of the gypsy who is coming to take away the caravan. Oh, but it is a beautiful piece of design! It is what those cool London types dream of, slightly askew Letraset on lined paper. It looks like Constant Brillant must come from the circus. I feel he can answer any need we have. Does he want to buy a barn?

When Monsieur Brillant comes and there is the manly noise of vehicles and negotiation, I hide in bed. The caravan goes. I ask James how it went.

'Well, he wanted money. I told him I didn't have any.'

Which is perfectly correct.

Oh, sun. A long day which must be the first real start of spring. The air so fragrant, you would never think that only the night before it had stunk of pigshit, in that thick, coated, let's-get-the-hell-out-of-here kind of way. Now it is silky and rich with birdsong. I spend all day sitting/lying on the new slate steps I made, the dry earth sticking to all my clothes. The lizards come by, and there are bees. In February. It is delightful. I rest and drink water. Joe comes out and covers some grass seed with earth: I fantasise wildly about wisteria.

It is light in the morning now, just, as I drive the kids to the school bus. Swathes of mist rise off the landscape, unveil this clear new day. I do an hour's work, then I walk up the track. The air is cold but you can feel the warmth coming through; young, early, fresh. The birds can't stop singing, a multitude of song. Music of the field birds – a high, sweet tune above them all. I don't know what bird it is, though I have heard it before. It is a very particular sound on a very particular day. It wipes out all thoughts of money or property, all the miniature machinations of the mind that constantly turns. It just is. It is not interested in future projections, or harking back, it just wants to be here and now. Delicious. Addictive. I just want to be in it. There are two or three small snowdrops and the daffodils will burst through any day now. Of the crocuses I planted, imagining some lush carpet of colour, there are small drops of purple and yellow on the bank beneath the oaks. Skylarks. Those birds – they're skylarks.

Greensward

The days start misty then build to a crescendo of sun, warm and rich. Birdsong is a cacophony. Days are long. The sky is a viscous painting of blue trails, pink and luminous in the morning. Yesterday, a leap day, we cleared out the attic. We had a conversation about it first, in which I grappled with emotional attachment to sofas. I want to keep them, battered old things that they are, and fix the small brown one. James wants to chuck them. We may come to a compromise and store them for now. We painted a quick mental image of the workshop emptied of most tools, with windows, the pool table and sofas around. And easels. Quite a picture.

James shifted loads of stuff from the dirty brown attic. Tiny fragments of metal, the large and the small all jumbled up any which way. The cardboard box of my 'office stuff' that had sat there so formidably actually didn't contain much at all and most of it went on the bonfire. Old tents, old paddling pools and so much more is loaded into the van ready to go to the *déchetterie*. I work at the computer all day.

There exists this 'inbetween' place, a sort of limbo while we disentangle ourselves from the French systems and before we realign ourselves with the British one. It would not be sensible to invest money we don't have on a building we are not going to be living in. I need to take that on board as a fact.

It is an odd state, because if you are living somewhere, as we are here, it seems strange not to make improvements. What makes it more pronounced is that, having made the decision to leave, we are not moving immediately. Rather, we are looking at rentals and planning a journey for me back to Britain. I will complete some work and find somewhere for us all to live. The timing for moving will hang off the availability of rentals.

We get the barn valued. Susie and her colleague come and do a thorough job, looking through all the paperwork, planning permissions and deeds. I think James was relieved to hear we might get back what we bought it for.

I go to Wales by train, for four days. Part work trip, part house-finding mission; each day is full. I look at dodgy overpriced workshops in Llanfairfechan, a caravan in Caernarfon, weighing up properties and prices around the area. Overall I wonder at the scrappy, small and narrow nature of Wales. A lot of pebbledash in the rain – how can I ever have thought this country was beautiful? The American students on the seats next to me say this is a beautiful country, and of course I guess it is, looking out at the green patchwork fields plus sheep. I feel distanced from it, different to how I used to feel, gazing out at Puffin island from the moving train.

I stay with my mum and Charles. Eternally kind, they drive me from place to place. We sit in an old-fashioned Llangefni café and read the property pages. We look in estate agents' windows and follow up leads on vacant rentals. This includes sad buildings that people can't sell, looking forlorn in Gwalchmai, and one grandiose farmhouse with five bedrooms. We spend time standing in sheds and cold yards, weighing up their size.

One morning we meet the Anglesey agent I have been emailing from France. I wear my cream trenchcoat which is woefully optimistic and wholly inappropriate for this chilly March day. Samantha drives me across country in her 4x4, with Charles and my mum in close pursuit. Sam shows us possible rentals: a house on a beach (workshop too small), a house with a dead hare in the driveway (workshop non-existent).

We drive down a long track to one house which has a good

stone outbuilding. James and I have seen this property online and earmarked it before I set off. It is in the middle of absolutely nowhere, but we liked the look of the outbuilding: secure and functional. It stands square on its own, with the workshop alongside. It has been newly renovated, there are still earthworks going on outside. Scrubby hawthorn scratches at us on the approach.

Sam shows us around. It is clean and newly decorated, these positive aspects my mum communicates to me *sotto voce* as we stand in the bathroom. There are three bedrooms, a decent workshop, a garden. It ticks all the boxes. It is in the middle of a 'shoot', so we would not be allowed cats or dogs. As we walk out to the cars, I walk a little down the track and catch sight of a small church in the field, a bell in its apex.

I take many photos and communicate all this information to James and the kids via email. Then I email Sam and tell her, yes, it is ideal and we would like to rent it.

Anglesey is the nearest I can get to wilderness, to a sense of space. We are lucky to be able to afford to move there. I will have to work hard. I must keep heart.

I travel further north, for my meeting. Britain is overcrowded, every patch of space claimed, sectioned off by large grey spiky metal fencing along the railside, keeping people IN and keeping people OUT. On the train journey to Manchester I compare the proximity of some terraced houses to the spacious horseland of Knutsford. There are a lot of boring houses, all the same.

I walk up the hill to Granny's house from the train station. I will stay here tonight and travel on in the morning. In this town young people eat as they're walking down the street, the pavements are stained with sick and spit and spilt takeaways. I sound middleclass, middleaged.

I am slightly fazed – at the finding of houses, at seeing so many people in so few days, at the imminent move. I feel the wrench away from a quiet way of life, one that is over too soon. How did it happen? What does it mean? I am tired, what with sleeping in other people's houses, travel, and the enormity of the work ahead. I know I am lucky, very fortunate, to be able to move at all, to a lovely house, and a job still there, ready and waiting.

At the moment I am trying to keep perspective on the freelance work – trying not to feel overwhelmed with the quantity and quality of the work I have to produce. There has been no time for concentrated work because of househunting. I tell myself when I get back home to the barn I will be able to get my head down. Don't panic.

The house in Anglesey is in a strange land, a strange place. Remote. We will fill it with liveliness and it will be fine.

I must just keep my head screwed on now until I get back to France. Keep my head screwed on in Premier Inn Barnsley Central. We may have a house in Wales in six weeks time. How strange is that, now that it has come? All the myriad things to do with timing, and school. All the cost. Blimey.

Back to the barn. James and Anna pick me up in the sunshine from Vannes station. It is ridiculous, but I feel guilty because I have found us somewhere to live in Wales, a house with a workshop. I feel I have betrayed the barn somehow, for feeling excited at new walls, rooms, white and gloss paint.

The glorious weather, the tulips exposed, full blown. Magnolia falling on the ground down by the pond. I don't know whether I am coming or going. I am neither here nor there. I want to be here, but can't invest any money on plants, and can't invest much imagination in a future for the barn – though that never stops, not really. A monastery, among other things. Or sell it. Consolidate. All too often I feel as though we should tighten up, get it right, be safe, secure, financially.

All this tumult of changing country, changing tax systems, it takes its toll. I tend to compare myself with other, more 'organised' people, and that does us absolutely no favours at all. We must rejoice in who and where and how we are now. Let that be my talking-to. And now I am off to buy some food for the kids. They got a *Félicitations* again, for 2nd trimester. So my feeling of being 'neither here nor there' can just go hang. I am here. I will be there. So it is.

Pretty much a perfect day, really. I work on words and images for a design feature. James is working full-tilt in the workshop, the sound of sawing. Doors lined up like pages on trestle tables in the sun, which spreads and extends from the morning birdsong right the way through to the long evening. There is a small routine of watering the new grass, watering the plants.

Anna and I go to buy stationery things from the shop in Locminé. I manage not to drive onto any concrete ramps. She is so on-form. We drive past the guy who lives by the roadside in his caravan. He always seems to be standing outside with his belly stuck out, gazing at the road: his domain. The tables outside his caravan are full of something – what? I try to make out what it is every time I pass by. Some sort of eco-decomposing arrangment. A garden. Or something.

James has told me what the shining things are: bottles.

'Look at all those bottles!' I exclaim to Anna, as we pass by.

'Yes, he must be one of those Arty farmers,' she says.

'Yes,' I say. 'He must.'

She is enjoying basketball, and we play on the concrete outside. It makes her laugh when I snatch the ball away from her. It makes her breathless.

The house in Anglesey has come through. So quick. So quick it seems it will all be over. Today I do not agonise about this, about uncertainty: I just enjoy the day. I read last night about the idea of compassion, and that money and materialism do not dominate all, we have to work not to let them. That struck a chord, because it justifies an alternative, non-financial-sense aspect to holding on to the barn.

I do wonder about how high the grass will grow again, and all the brambles. How quickly something goes when untended. But today I think it is possible, that it is enjoyable, that it is part of it – how I keep fit, pulling brambles endlessly. The re-balance of teaching and British life, managing to keep it in check. Today. I am wearing a long stripey cotton dress. Joe has a new haircut. Anna and I have been translating work about ancient Greece for her test tomorrow. Their eyes are bright and shiny. I feel fine.

What has the barn taught us? I think of that while I consider again how putting it on the market would be. It seems clear to me today that it should be so, that the dream has to be broken, without continuation. It is what it is; it was what it was. Time to move on. If renting in Britain is not cost-effective over time, then buying in Britain is the only alternative.

Here in the barn, we have so few outgoings. Even in this context we find it hard to get by. There is infinite pleasure though in managing to exist on very little, and this is something I want to try to take with me. We will not be living in this country, so why keep the barn on? It is not as though we will have an excess of funds in order to build it, and to travel to it will only continue to be costly. So perhaps it is time to bite the bullet. For all the beautiful land and birds and peace and space, it is not viable: that has been shown. Maybe in six years or so, when the kids have left school, but even then the cost of travel remains.

Perhaps it is time for me to get real, to try again to find somewhere we can live quietly, simply and affordably. Surely it should not be so difficult in the outback of Anglesey. If we put the barn on the market, and one day sell it, then there is a clarity of location, at least. One country. One family home unit, that can absorb our energies as a continuum.

After two hours working at the computer – it feels like one – I am writing about the History of Print. I complete the section then hang out the washing and walk up the track. I am aware how fortunate I am, because where else have I found this freedom – to be able to write, about things I enjoy, in the middle of the day. And as I walk up the track I imagine women's voices, saying, *Hang on to it, Jane.* I imagine how I would advise someone else. There are two parts to every story, two sides to the coin. It is strange how we can hold these different concepts in our mind at the same time.

But there it is. The fortune I've found in my own daily life is due to this chain of events, this particular place and time, which has not happened by chance but has been created by us. I'm not sure that it is even repeatable – if we came here to live as older folk, would we really be arsed about getting the satellite internet sorted out, finding work, making it work? Perhaps this time is just simply *this* time; this favourable experience, walking up a track in the end of March breeze, the new green lines of the mown field. Greensward of my own, after so many years of playing in the park, or hankering after other people's gardens.

This has shown me that the things I thought I enjoyed – planting, gardening, gazing into the middle distance, sunshine, are truly the things I enjoy. I will hang on to them and cultivate them consciously in life. I want more of that.

I remember being a disposessed seventeen-year-old, living all over the place, yearning for two weeks on my own in Val's little cottage, 'to paint'. Quiet is what I wanted. Peace. This place gives me that, under unsustainable circumstances, it turns out, but I wouldn't change it for anything. How do you recreate this same thing in Britain? *Can* you recreate this in Britain? Owning a place, even a stone barn, gives you a sense of calm, knowing that there is no-one to pay, no money to earn except to get by. No big cash. James would say that is an illusion, that the French system has big payments, same as Britain, and he is right. I can see that. I've experienced that.

The sun continues to shine, day after day. James and I have a routine of bread, fish and cheese for lunch. It's 23 degrees in the shade on Ange's thermometer. Dunno what it is in the sun, but it's darned hot out there. High summer.

We have bought Joe a guitar for his birthday. He made a lemon cake last night with Dad and has taken that to school today for their communal cake stall. Anna has basketball today, which she enjoys and is good at. She got another great mark in maths recently and another *Encouragement* in her school report.

I am going peasant-brown inbetween learning about William Morris, early publishing and that old weirdo Mr Gill. I lie on the south bank steps reading about Morris and the rest of the art gang – Fauvists, Futurists, Dadaists, Constructivists. It inspires me in the ways of eccentric and radical art ideas, going against conventions. Artists in the full scope of the term – painting, printing, making, sculpting: Cool. It is a perfect day. Life is very full, like this. I think of planting a formal row of those damned palm laurels, so that one day they make a stand and cast some shade on the lawn. I reassure myself I will do this more, it is not the End of something, of finding this creative enjoyment, but merely the beginning.

Vinca Major

WOOD ANEMONE
CELANDINE
VETCH
BLUEBELL
VIOLET

Cream and brown through the upright trees – misty patches of trunk and fragmented cows on the opposite bank, like a crazy jigsaw puzzle. Tiny budding leaves just beginning, on elders and other plants; climbers, that I can't possibly know the names of. The field of formal trees starting to blossom, soon it will be in full bloom, the bluebells intoxicating, then I won't know what to do with myself. The magnolia already falls like lotus blossom by the *maire*'s pond, an everyday meditation as we drive up the track.

I take a backpack and walk with purpose, as though I am not really pillaging the land for small flowers, though there is nobody watching, no one *to* watch, and even if there was, I doubt they would care. I think about the hunters as I dig a small clump of anemone down by the river. I walk out a circle of east, south, west, north and back to east again. I draw it later in my sketchbook and understand what a mandala might be.

Celandine = easy.

Bluebell = 1 bulb.

Vetch = unable to tell where the root is.

Violet = the first small clump. I scatter leaf litter to hide my tracks.

A small *cache*, but on the way back, a feeling of guilt and shame at doing something 'wrong'. Uprooting these plants makes me think about Mum being told off by a prominent local author for collecting wild flowers. Not that I was there, but the heat of indignation, shame and knowledge of being in the wrong makes me blush. My hands are florid and I rest them on an elder branch to take the heat out of them. I move my palms up the woody trunk to a cooler, smoother patch. It does the job.

In the early afternoon I go to a *Vive Le Jardin* in the centre of town, in the ancient *presbytère*. Maryvonne gives me two boxes of all sorts of plants; I don't know what they are, but I stick 'em in the soil. Some will live and some will die, no doubt.

In the late afternoon the track is lined with thirty or more cars and vans – they keep on coming, parking on the grass verge. The people turn into a brass band on the brown ploughed field. The Hunter's jamboree.

Like the last one to leave the party, eventually it dawns on me. James and I talk, sitting on the steps on the south bank, with the dry brown earth I love so much.

'I'm worried about you, planting all these plants, when there won't be anyone here to look after them,' he says.

It makes me quiet. I lie awake at night, thinking about it. In looking *forward,* to a new home, you have to release the old. Keeping the old on is confusing. Not just in, *what objects do we take?* practical sort of confusing, but in the wider psychological aspect. Having duality would lead to unhappiness, really – we would be neither there, properly, nor here, properly. We have done a lot of that.

We do not have enough money to build it. We do not intend to live here. There is not really any benefit in 'hanging on' to it in case we want to come back in the future. So there it is.

James says, 'Yes: put it on the market. No more debate.'

It will free the path to clarity: to Britain and all its challenges. One place, one household. No to-ing and fro-ing. None of the inherent cost and continuous confusion.

Didn't sleep. Frost leads to warm sun. I pop up to *la poste* and the *boulangerie*, and am sad then that it will be done and gone, just as I can order two baguettes with authority and conviction. I tell myself sternly that there is more to life than ordering bread, but I think, who else would this living suit – this life, this barn?

Susan and her colleague come over again this afternoon to take photos and look at the deeds. The barn may not sell for a long time of course, in which case my desires for easels in the workshop may well happen. But it will always be impermanent now, because sense has won out – the need to make a living, as simply as possible, in one country.

If I was ever giving advice to anybody thinking of doing this, I would say: Do It. But do it now, while you are thinking of it. Clear the path for it and do it wholeheartedly, while the children are little. And for me, I would say; do not look back, overmuch, and do not look forward, either, too much. There is no Then, there is only Now. Right here. Enjoy it while you can. Relish it, treasure it. All the ideas and hopes pinned to this country and this barn – they did not all come true. But some of them did – we are here, we are happy, we are whole. In the long term, it may not be financially prudent to try to sustain it. It is choice. And energy. And reality – you have to protect yourself against the cold dark days, even though the sun shines. It is a small mirage, sometimes, this place.

I think the barn may take a year or two to sell, by which time we will be fed up with paying rent. We may even have bought a field in the interim, and be caravan or tipi-dwellers. Anything is possible now. The freedom that owning a patch of land gives you is something I had not experienced before, and it is as rich and pleasant as I thought it would be. Being close to nature.

So I need to Learn from this shit, in every holistic way – money-wise, career-wise, family-wise. What is important to me and what are the needs of our family? I think I am better placed to answer those questions now, with some conviction and authority; a bigger mission than buying a baguette.

Well, there it is online, at 7.50am this morning: *grange à rénover.* The pictures make it look fine; red-tile roof, grass all around. It has the glamour of new photos of your own house that make you want to hang onto it. When I look at the extent of it, the length and the familiar features, I still see exactly how it could look, fully renovated with windows and doors leading to the outside.

So there is a sadness. Sadness at closing it, mingled sweet sadness, and a thin vein of wondering if we are doing the right thing. But this is dominated by a much harder, clearer sight. It just wasn't meant to be. I guess that's how you say it. *Nous n'avons pas le finance*, that is the reality of it. We have had it for six years (to the day) and we have talked it all around. I am sorry for many things, but these cannot hang on to my ankle in the future. It has to be let go. It has to be a fresh start, armed hopefully with some sort of wisdom.

I am ready to go now. All day I've known it. It will be strange, to think of this place when it is a beautiful day and there is no-one here. It is strange, knowing I am ready to go – I want the journey, want to know that it is going to happen, want to know When. Want it kind of Now. It has been a slow day, but okay. Both James and I know this is a kind of superficial life, especially for the children, though they don't seem to mind anything too much. It is a transition period.

The bluebells are coming up and it is going to be splendid. Joe and I walk along the river. The fragrance is amazing, and I don't know where it comes from. I sniff every plant I suspect. If I knew what it was I would buy loads of it and have it, always.

The things that make me know I am moving are when I look at objects that happen to have come together, sentimental small things that make a home, and imagine them moving out. At the moment it is a tin lantern, a small wooden horse and a Venus of

Willendorf figurine that sits on the bookshelf in our bedroom. It will be easy to pack this time, I think. I will just throw everything into the hamper, suitcases, and Go. I am looking forward to it. I imagine life inside our new home, and I think it is important to look forward to something.

It is a difficult couple of days, I think maybe some of the hardest yet. I am impatient; I think of every way to go. James is under pressure with the job he has to finish, the kids are on school holidays with nothing much to do. Not great combinations, but I think we are out of it now. No-one lost their temper. It is raining, but we have been on a beach trip to Quiberon and out shopping for goodies for Joe's birthday.

It feels like coming down a mountain – in that it can be more dangerous than going up. Easier to make mistakes when your knees are wobbly and loose, and all the constraints have gone. There is no dangling carrot, nothing to strive for, that keeps your energy focused and intact, as it does on the way up. We need to stay strong now, perhaps more than ever, as the last few weeks play out. There are lots of decisions to make – about the exact date we go, the kids' last day at school, all that stuff. Susan is bringing a client round to view the barn early on Saturday morning, so we'll make ourselves scarce.

I feel as though I am being Shown a Lesson, and it is lasting as long as it takes me to understand that it has to be learnt, absorbed, become part of me. It is something to do with standing by family, by being patient, by being active, by being clear. It is something to do with recognising what is important and real to me. It is about accepting some things and rejecting others.

Living like this has shown me how I love these people, and how wonderful they are. In a small space, within a shed, we have lived properly and well. It is not Perfect nor Ideal, because life isn't. I have been fearful the last few days, unknown fears or fears of the absolute. Fear of ending here without making it back, not being able to envisage the van starting, that sort of thing. Concrete activity like signing the Tenancy agreement focused me. It will be alright, I tell myself. It will not be easy, this next week, but we will get through it. People deal with a lot worse.

Joe's birthday went okay, I made big pots of *moules marinière*. James goes out to work, me and the kids decamp to St Nicholas while Susan shows the client around the barn. Later, she calls to say they would like to re-visit tomorrow afternoon. Explained to the kids we had put barn on market. Easily accepted, Joe and Anna in good spirits. Showery rain and I'm trying to do a little work. I feel better for even doing a little.

Joe and I go for a short walk. I try to lift my heart on the way back. I think of the phrases 'light-hearted' and 'heavy-hearted'. I can't currently find my heart. I think I have Lost Heart. This would seem to be borne out by the lack-lustre way in which I approach the day(s). I should count my blessings more.

The weather is windy and showery – any sun there is I rush out to lie in, but it's cold. I can't seem to find any peace – I don't feel any affinity with anything much, my old days of finding love in it all seem gone. I see objectively how easy it must be for people to begin to 'hate' France and French living. I begin to begrudge Ange coming to the barn every day, the routine sound of his car, the routine sounds of kids, people. Maybe I begrudge them their 'belonging' – their innate right to be here.

Yesterday evening I went for another walk with Joe along the river after dinner. I felt some energy coming back to me, and every thump of the stick on the ground had a gratifying wholesome resonance which brought me back into myself. The phrase 'your heart isn't in it' is such an unhappy thing to experience, and it is always horrible to witness somebody falling apart, particularly when it's yourself you observe. So I began to get my dander up a little.

The kids back to school after Easter hols. The rain makes the track shine like a silver snake between the fields of wet brown earth, light off the back of a seagull as it flies up along the edge of the field. I think about a triumvirate:

GREED
VANITY
EGO

and how these have informed my decision-making in life.

I thought about my past, how I have felt like a tin can bashed about. The other evening I sat on the green chair in the bathroom and followed this thread all the way back, right to the beginning, and then unraveled it again, so that it made perfect sense. I thought I had worked it all out before, but I had to follow it back again. And this time it was all the way back. This time it was not fixated on things that had 'gone wrong' – my anger, upset and confusion, and the repercussions – but was about my interpretation of them *now*.

And it came to me that the tight caucus I have about my mistake and my guilt, can be let go. I can *forgive* myself. Actively forgive myself. I can allow myself to understand that it was not all bad. Though there were things that I need to pay heed to, in order not to repeat them – important things to do with where I place my energy and how – but life has shown me some things. It is important to be able to let the past go. I will work to let it go.

I do not mean that I intend to sail through the remainder without conscience, but more a gentle allowance, a gentility. A kindness. A forgiveness. To work on that towards others, and to myself. Maybe this is possible, now that we have reached this balance. We make mistakes. Both of us do. We can count them up, and we have done. But in order to go forward, you have to be kind to yourself, in some part. We can't castigate ourselves for ever. This has been the coming out of it, the healing of it, the realisation of it. And we can go on now, with the death of this place. The conscious cutting of the ideal. And the insight into what the ideal is, in our hearts.

Does it matter to me that we have not built our Dream House and are not living our Dream Life in France? Fundamentally, no: it has not broken my heart. It is a shame, in many ways – mainly the non-realisation of a creative vision of the building. But it has brought to light the realities of what that involves in terms of finance and there is a pragmatism in that. We do not have the money, nor are we willing to borrow it. Some people do have the money, or an element of it, and have had a different consciousness in how they have approached it. I would not change my consciousness for theirs, because that is to swap my soul, and I value it, and my husband's, too highly now.

Another reason it does not break my heart is that I do not need convincing of our skills, or James's prowess, in terms of making things or craftsmanship. We live here. We live like this, with the fire burning wood, good food on the table and a quality in our familial relationships. We have paid work, doing what we are good at.

I walked into the workshop the other day and James was sanding the length of a handrail for a staircase. He says he works 'like a ghost' now, that all the creativity has gone out of it. That may be so, but I still know that every piece of work he makes has a value and integrity embedded into it. He cannot help it. So the energy that goes into that handrail, so swift, is a good energy, for a longstanding thing that has inherent value. That is important, and that does not go. That is the blueprint on your soul.

Of course the barn outside this room is a mess. The middle and end barn have disparate pieces of wood and metal and rubble in them. Holes in the floor, no roof. And it feels bad to leave it like that, to try to sell it like that. The impulse – one impulse – is to tidy it up, to clear the decks a little, so that anyone looking at it has a clear canvas. That is one impulse. The other impulse is to just walk away from it, to hide from it. I know that we will tidy it up a little. Shovel the rubble into the holes in the floor.

It is about cutting the cord. It is not necessary to idealise the flowers, the stones, because we are not putting our emotional investment in that any more. Consequently the things look sad. That is partly where the care is going to have to come in – the practical care. When we start pulling this place apart and moving stuff – beds, washing machine, table – and the inevitable disarray that ensues, we are going to have to be careful that we leave it tidy, that we tie up loose ends. Because saying goodbye is as important as greeting, the way you say goodbye is as important as saying hello – the letting something in, the entrance, is more exciting and full of possibility. But in this case, as the exit is made the new beginning begins. It has never felt more like that.

And I am not heartbroken because we are going back to a place where I come from, where the language and landscape are familiar and old. This time I will go there older and wiser, I think the phrase is. Those phrases are coming thick and fast.

I am wise enough to know that the right answer will evolve over time. To trust in myself that I – we – will make the right decision, right for us. No more anger, no more fear. I feel more solid in stating my choices now.

The challenge will be to find the balance within the relationship between home life, work life and the means to pay for it all. That is my small quest and it is one I will approach with care, eyes open to all the ramifications. For example, would the freedom of more creative time (i.e. time not spent lecturing) outweigh the reduced income?

It is a new beginning. A new life. A new arrangment, new responsibilities. A re-balance, perhaps for me to be more aware of the importance of softness and the real things of life, of care, of quietness. Of perhaps not working every bloody day like a machine, being prepared to forfeit some worldly financial cash for the health benefits of that.

James is at work in Josselin and will be working there now until it is done. We have set a date for moving and will inform the school and the children this week. We leave on 15th May, a Tuesday. So a new patch of movement will come soon.

We went to Vannes market, Anna and I. We rose early on the Saturday morning and set off, loading up with petrol and lots of cash. I was paid for a job, so the money burnt a hole in my pocket. In the end, we did not buy anything: the black linen skirt is still in the shop and I don't really miss it.

We walked down through the town; fresh wind, some sun, Anna so *chic* in her indigo jacket and domed pink plastic umbrella. The market was a crush of people, men in good jumpers, carrying poodles. Stalls piled with lemons, honey and onions, hats, scarves, and stripey Breton jumpers. Freesias going into baskets. For once I felt I was absolutely in the right place at the right time, that this was where it was happening; this was where it was at.

We bought baguettes, Sprite and cookies at the *boulangerie* at the bottom of the hill by the gate, past the kitchen and apron shop. I felt glad we were not going to buy an expensive restaurant lunch. The *boulangerie* was crammed and again I felt like we were doing the right thing. We sat on the quay, in that pale-blue and creamy light next to the boats, with the merry-go-round under the trees in the distance, the half-timbered houses in sage green and yellow ochre. Such colours and all the people, with their scooters and pooches and French style. I thought to myself then that Llangefni hasn't got quite the same thing, and of course Wales has not. It is a different climate altogether, that's the way it is.

It has been wetter and colder, the bluebells that I thought would bloom so quickly have been longer and slower. The magnolia lotus blossom tulip tree has had its petals bashed and stymied by the weather. Along the river track the fragrance and aroma of *that* plant is still an intoxicant. It's cherry blossom, James and I decided. A single flower gives only a hint, the slightest indication of it, but *en masse* it must be the source.

The river runs full and high – only the tip of the island is visible. It flows fast. Down there the wind isn't strong, so we get to see things differently from up at the barn where the wind bangs around all day. The water is bright and earth-coloured, the branches hang over and into it, leaves reflected brown against the lighter shades of sky. There are fast swirls and eddies, white bubbles float away. The leaf shapes echo the bubbles, the wind running through it all. I do three sun salutations, and look up into the branches of the oak high above, dark against the sky. Small white petals on dark earth underfoot, pussywillow like full, fat, lime caterpillars.

The slim tree trunks in the field, pale like that Piero della Francesca painting – I remember dragging Joe to see it at the National Gallery. Our walk is uplifting, it blows away the stasis. I remember I should do yoga, make it part of my day – it is important to put that perspective on things. I remember then – when I am getting excited about the trees and the river and the light and the colour and how I could ever explain them – I remember the polar opposites of being exciteable and dull. I remember what I was thinking about the other day, about victimhood and glamourisation, the need to take the middle way. Finding a balance.

I need to actively build in the things which I know make me feel fulfilled, whole, with a healthy, forgiving nature. These are:

Yoga.

Gardening.

Walking.

I would like to keep hens.

So those things have to come into my life, much more. I have to MAKE them come into my life, much more, by doing them.

The other day me and the kids walked upriver along the other side, the opposite direction to our usual route. We walked a hidden path, cuved and windy, on the river's edge. The ground was a carpet of Vinca major, purple flowers on glossy green leaves.

I think about uprooting my plants, taking them with me. They are a straggly interruption, those laurel *palmiers*, but the rhodos, lavender and others might have to come. The rosemary, certainly, the small shrubs too. Or perhaps I will leave them. It would be strange uprooting them and of course they are not a priority.

The kids are on strange timetables at school, which enlivens them. Right now they are sitting at and on the kitchen table, listening to Joe's ipod. Sometimes after school Joe hangs out with his friends – Vincent, Aurélie and the others – at Baud park. They make smoke bombs, play football and ride about the town on bikes. Sometimes they go to Miguel's house and his mum makes them french fries.

I make fishfinger sandwiches, write to the accountant, do a little work and shopping. I have booked ferry tickets back and contacted the school. Still much to do. It is not pretty, this French tax stuff, but it is not out of hand. We have done it all properly, as well as we can, in good faith. We are not hiding from our responsibilities: we will tidy it all up. I have to remind myself that if we had never signed up for this – French life, French tax, we may have been idealising and hankering after it without actually experiencing the reality of it. The lines you hear: *The French respect artisans. The French tax system is more lenient on artisans if you have 3 children.*

It is all bollocks, really. It is expensive, same as anywhere else. The landscape is big and wide, the culture is upright, self-regarding and I like a lot of it.

Right now the clouds are dark and full but the land is bathed in sunlight: that dramatic contrast. I have to actively facilitate the Flow of Good Stuff through my life. This means, no sneaking sugar in my tea – fat and flabby. It means actively thumping my walking stick against the ground when I need to bang some sense through the earth up into my soul. To rid myself of trivia, unhealthy thoughts and anxieties.

It means to train my mind out of those bad thoughts that are based on jealousy, resentment or sadness. Away they go. On the air. Down the river. Anywhere except within me. I have no room for them. They take up too much space which is too valuable, too precious. Like a car lot – those feelings or thoughts are like a carpark outside Matalan, which is absolutely inappropriate. I am creating a green area, near water, which is full of life.

Férié

Accounts. In order. Good news from the accountant and not as bad as we thought regarding how much dosh has to go out. We receive the keys to the new house. I am pleased and slightly bovine, which always makes the kids happy. It is *férié*, so nothing is open and it is apparently the only day in France when no newspapers are printed. I play chess with Joe – I even *win,* much to his disgruntlement.

Anna gives me a makeover sitting outside in the sun. Green eyeshadow, she leans in to do the dark purple eyeliner. I see her face very close up, hair hanging around her green eyes, with a host of seagulls in the sky behind. The tractor burns up and down the fields, spraying shit. I don't know why the seagulls should like that so much, but they do. The tractor stops periodically on the brow of the hill, a silhouette like a child's drawing.

As Joe and I play chess on a small table we've set up on the glossy grass where the caravan used to be, the *maire*'s wife walks past and comes over slowly in her big padded coat. She has had an operation and is recovering. Joe is polite and French and it is only much later, as I cycle up along the top road (braving the dogs, but there are none) that I realise I am still wearing the crazy-lady make-up. 'Hideous', Joe calls it. That, and my American tan popsocks, just about do it.

White cat, brown field, early morning. Apple blossom on new trees. An incredible dream. Siddhartha-like James, flowing river, round pool and staircase, tea-towel prayer flags and a decision made. Writing, everyone out at college and work.

Van in garage, won't start. Dodgy computer. Have to delay crossing – bit messy, but unavoidable. James finishing up the job, drizzly day trying to work out logistics. A lot of stress.

Kids' last week at school. End of an era, I realise, as I walk up the track early this morning, before I sit down and work. No more days with that routine, early up and out, then a clear day ahead for me. I take a cup of coffee up the track and look at the plants as I go, in my wellies and skirt. The woodpigeons are cooing, grass is lush and wet. The rhododendron is carmine red, a luxury. Lily of the valley in a bunch on the sink, a gift from Maryvonne at French class last night, to celebrate. No class next week as *Ascension*. No class for me as Leaving.

The kids have bought sweets and gifts to share with their friends. They exchange letters, bracelets, toys and photos. They are happy. There will be a week where they don't go to school here and we get ready. A natural break from one system to another.

Are you excited or a bit sad? my friend Simone texts.

I feel a bit stunned, more than anything. I feel as though I am on a wave, riding over this massive upheaval. A bit sad, yes. But also not-a-bit-sad, because I see how the children have benefited, how I have benefited, from this time. Joe is tall and speaking Spanish at the dinnertable. Anna is composed and sweet, same as she ever was, but more so. I don't know what I am. A bit dishevelled certainly, but nothing a makeover wouldn't fix.

A couple of full sun days. Planes traversing completely blue sky. So many of them, they must come out cos it's May. I lie sheltered next to the rabbit-run on a patch of velvety green grass, in my bikini. I am only allowed to wear my bikini when the children are not around. I do some work. I do very little in the way of cooking. I read reports and send off the files I've written. I think about new openings: if I can make it work, I will. I think about balance: what constitutes value and what necessity.

I sorted through crockery yesterday, in the sunshine, washing off the cobwebs and mouse shit. I became stuck at nana's sherry glasses on the table, next to some mismatched plates. Where do they go? What do I do with them? Do they live *there* or *here*? They are not in the Necessity category (the stuff which goes first) but obviously they are sacred, must be sacred, because I can still remember the kitchen cupboard in which they lived, all those years. Lined with wallpaper, behind the chair, which meant it was always difficult to open the door.

Nana's kitchen cupboard. These glasses that were used at Christmas and New Year, small phials of coloured liquid. Exotic, in the same way that Babycham glasses were. A different time, *The Two Ronnies*, electric fire and a fug of home comfort. The glasses get put into a tin and will end up in the back of some cupboard in the new kitchen. Inevitable.

Now there are suitcases in the workshop, which has become a sort of holding bay. Anna and Joe are emptying out their rooms in good spirits. It is happening, transit time, with its own particular momentum. Joe shifted the rubble in the middle barn and I swept it. We played chess outside as the weather turned, the wind picked up and he checkmated me, against all the odds, swiftly. I find in chess I start really well and then get impatient and try to force the end, so I lose focus on the long haul, eager to get to the kill. I never win that way. It is pure luck on my part, a lot of it, but I beat him more now than I used to.

Playing chess reminds me of that time Simone and I stayed in Penzance. Mike, a man we met blind drunk at a disco and went to stay with for three weeks. No monkey business. Simone made hamburgers and we lay in the garden a lot, me drawing. It reminds me of time suspended with nothing urgent to do, no place to be except here, playing chess in the sun. And when it clouds over and gets a bit chilly, finding a jumper, bringing in the rugs, that sort of thing.

My overdraft is massive, which stops me going anywhere or buying anything except two baguettes. My life is richer for it.

Lay awake and couldn't sleep. *Penzance*! I thought. And I remembered the photo that exists somewhere of a fifteen-year-old me, standing at the sign at John o' Groats. We hitch-hiked from the top of the country to the bottom, as fast as we could. It was 'something to do'. Was I fifteen then? That would make me a year older than Joe is now. How can that work? Penzance is a thread, a handhold to times and dates that have all been a jumble for me up until now. I can trace summers, schools and art college and it gives me some clarity.

Moving. James shifting stuff. Took the kids to meet Bea in Malestroit – they will stay over one night while James and I dismantle beds. Discuss taking the cooker and the fridge. I stand around like a spare part. Wash cutlery, put things in boxes. Wonder how it is all going to fit in. James's Zen van-packing, everything in its place. Boots wedged in corners – I know the drill now; I know how it will unpack at the other side. I begin to feel anxious, but I plant some cuttings Bea gave me – wisteria and roses – God knows if they'll survive. I take a walk in the late evening and see that the yellow plant I thought may have been dead, is not dead but *is* my very favourite scented azalea.

The big rhodos with sticky buds will come out when we are not here, ripe red and deep. The grass will need cutting – the grass will always need cutting. I will do what I can before we go, but there will always be stuff I will want to do. The house is emptier, sparse, and I remind myself before I get too sad that this is a flux, an in-between. Life goes on. We will see what happens. I walk up the track and the air is fine. The van is fixed, the crossing booked.

Evening light. We have packed the regular dinnertable so we eat on the old oak bench salvaged from the vestry. James calls the bench 'Like something from an orphanage, or prison'.

I say it is like a Hampstead noodle bar.

Van is backed up against the double doors, packed tight and

going to be tighter. Mattresses, cooker and fridge to go in next. And the rabbit hutch.

Joe and I walk by the river. He names the flowers and works out what GCSEs he'll choose back in Welsh school. Anna was not herself after coming back from Bea's. When I ask her what's up, she says she is tired of saying goodbyes – in Wales, in France, to Bea. Poor little mite. But my heart doesn't break, because we are going back, and she will be happy there on home turf, Welsh girl that she is. But French girl too, and good at it. Perhaps it is a small message to me that all may not be easy back in Britain, it will have its challenges. Setting up a new home, making it a home, when it is, after all, in the middle of bloody nowhere. I will have to enlist Anna's help with home-making. I will have to be alert to the influences that can make her fundamentally unhappy. I will exert authority when I have to. I will keep a close monitoring eye on how it is. We will not be too strict, but neither will I be as *laissez faire* as I was before. That's just how it is and will be. James has worked hard to pack the van. Early night, with *Tom Sawyer* in bed (not literally, obv).

The boot of my car is filled with: Monopoly, Risk, Cranium, Pictionary and Scrabble. It has a pair of boots, sandals, a red plantpot, spade and trowel and some small geranium plants in plastic bags, shoved in a silver bathroom bin. A tub of pegs. A tin of paints. There will be more, and at some point it will go over the 'tipping point' where organisation meets chaos and everything gets thrown in. Today the mattresses, fridge, oven and Mr Rufus get packed. Tomorrow morning our bedding, then that's it.

When Joe and I walked along the river he said, 'Look, you can't see the other side now.'

He's right, the leaves are so full that only glimpses of the river can be seen at the bottom of the incline, let alone the bank on the other side. The leaves have come out, almost imperceptibly at first, until they found their footing and now BLAM! It is all green.

Joe asks, 'What's *in* Anglesey?'

Bugger all, essentially, which is why I think I might like it.

'The rock is the oldest in the world,' I say.

It is the best I can manage.

I think about Bohemianism, as I do the washing up. It wins out over *bourgeois*.

I am glad I managed to get the small tasks done. I bought a Breton shirt and that black linen skirt, for forthcoming work. I am glad we got them safely, and the stuff from Lidl, it felt precarious somehow, in the rain.

I finish *Tom Sawyer* and think about Huck Finn, unhappy at having financial wealth and making his way back to his rags and freedom. I think about how I feel and I know I am calmer. More 'in myself'. I don't feel angry anymore. I feel that if things come along, which they will, I will deal with them, and with good heart. *Bonne volonté*, as they say.

I don't know what will happen or what we'll do with the barn – I can't know everything. I know my next job is to make a home for us all, work at making an echoey house homely for the kids. Work at staying sane, myself. I think the competitivism and general chatter of Britain might try to do me in. I have realised that peace is healthier and better for me than chatter. That perhaps peace and freedom are more valuable than money. Perhaps it is a more valuable thing to strive for, in this life. I won't turn my head to the needs of money and all the Stuff we will have to afford, but neither should I forget that you have to fight equally to factor in the good and important things in life – the gardening, walking, gawping and thinking.

Early, we set off. Cold misty day. The car starts. The van starts. We board up the kitchen window and lock the door. The barn turns into a derelict.

We drive, me and the kids in the car, following the van nose to tail. We're making good time. I notice the back wheel of the van looks wobbly as we pull in for coffee. Van tyre blows out just past

Plumelec. We pull over. Hazard lights. Fluorescent jackets. Cars speed past. James manages to jack the van up, it leans precariously.

'Do not get out of the car under any circumstances,' I tell the kids, as I get out to help him. The traffic zips past remorselessly.

We lift out Anna's heavy mattress and some framed paintings in order to get at the spare tyre. Our belongings come out of the van onto the hard shoulder, the greasy side of the cooker laid bare to the passing motorists. It could not be more of a predicament. I stand, not really being useful but trying to be supportive, propping things up as James manages to sort it out. He is calm, practical, he works fast. Cold fingers, there is blood on his hand. I think I will always remember this moment. Whenever I am in a bad mood with him, I will only have to think of this moment to remind myself what he is made of.

I drive behind him all the way to the ferry, watching that back wheel and hoping that it will not happen again. I tell myself it is time to be positive now, that the 'bad thing' has happened, bad luck will not strike twice. I am a bit shaky, but we plough on, up past Avranches and Mont Saint-Michel, up past Caen. Over the crazy bridges, which aren't as bad as the first time round, though they still look like something out of a seventies disaster movie. Anna is my co-pilot, she is like a lark. The back seat is now full of all the stuff we have de-camped from the van – guitar, duvets, baskets of food, boots. Joe is up with his dad in the van.

We get on the ferry. It is full of big male bikers, sprawled like walruses over all the comfy seats. We find the empty cinema room, a quiet refuge. It is cool and only a couple of sleeping oldies in there. Later on the peace is incredibly shattered by a family with young kids. The mum is loud and drinking wine, she has a big cleavage and a tattoo on her neck. Anna is fascinated, she thinks the mum is 'great'. I think the mum is astonishingly brilliant in her crassness. It is as though nothing is sacred. She either does not see, or has no heed, that this room is a Quiet Zone, the only one on the boat. All those people who are trying to sleep turn their heads, you can feel the general 'tut' of the company.

We come into Portsmouth in the sun, Anna on deck chattering away. We drive then, and I realise how tired I am as we overtake a lorry just on the M3 intersection. I am driving too fast, trying to keep up with James. We stop at Sutton Scotney. I am so tired that when I try to sleep it is only snatches of bad dream, with broken-down van and the like. But I do sleep, and when we wake up it is bright and I am grateful for clean white sheets.

We reach the next service station early enough for James's satisfaction. The roads are aggressive. I think about machismo, trucks, middle-aged men with middle-aged spreads, sales and business whizzes zooming up the fast lane. Everybody busy, everybody better than everybody else. Trucks do not like me, because I am following James at a slowish pace, when I could, of course, go much faster, or let them in. Birmingham is mental and long.

We drive through and over the mountains and arrive on Anglesey. By the time I manage to find the turning for the house, everyone has had enough. I hope that they like it. The track is narrow, but the van fits down it and comes to a halt.

It takes time to walk around, to unpack things, to get beds in. It is a lovely house.

'It is a big house! You didn't say it was a big house,' says James.

It is a big house – it didn't seem quite so big in March in the cold mist. But now the sun is shining, the rooms are clean and light, and it is a glorious house. It is completely peaceful, with only the birds tweeting.

Hawthorn

July 2012

It is funny, but it seems we have found our idyll in this place. Certainly I would never choose to live anywhere else. Over the last couple of days James and I have wondered about renting, the costs and principle of it. We do not mind paying a big rent for this place because it is, actually, fantastic.

It is more remote than I thought, so a fair drive in to school: it will cost in petrol. The internet dongle doesn't work, because the coverage is patchy. So we'll have to sign up for BT, which I was hoping to avoid. All the costs will start coming in, all the money is going out, like water. The little things we didn't bring for want of space, I am determined we will not buy again – cutlery drawer, waste paper basket, dish rack – that sort of stuff.

Asda. The women are bigger, floppy trousers and summer tops, chiffon to skim the plump. Hips, bums, boobs, arms, necks, cheeks. 'Smart' clothes, high heels, treated hair. Somehow they all look the same. The clothes hang with 'Jubilee' and 'Made in Britain' branding. Cheap material, pastel colours, big sizes. Everyone seems more agitated than in France. More people, more cars. I find that I tire very easily. Kids are at my mum's, Anna camping with Eleri. I am going to dig the veg patch.

My diary was filled with things like 'ring BT', 'bins', 'library', 'rugby shirt for Joe', and all these things got done. But how nice that they did not all get done on the day they were supposed to. It was sunny, the kids were at school and didn't need picking up. We did some shopping in an insanely huge Tesco and then walked along Trearddur bay. Later we sunbathed and did some drawing, then went for a swim in Rhosneigr. It was so good. It was how rich people live, we said to each other.

Hawthorn blossom thick like honeydew encircling the house. Creamy-blue pearlised light in the bedroom window, morning and night. Thick pile carpet, quiet underfoot.

I married a carpenter – I think of this as something to give this story context – a passage at the beginning, which explains needing to move for a workshop space, and the principles of being a perfectionist carpenter, a craftsman rather than a chippy. I see vans around Llangefni, local companies with Carpenters and Joiners in lettering on the side – the sort of advertising which James has never done and never will. How do they make it work? Piecemeal, I bet. It has to be businesslike and competitive; James is at a changing point now – it may be an end to commercial carpentry.

Freelance work continues apace, before I start back at the lecturing job. I struggle with the pace of it all. I talk to female colleagues on work trips up and down the country. They are tired, irritable, overworked. I think of 'dry crispbread women.' This has to be said in Sally's big Brummie accent. A couple of years ago I was being observed in my teaching role by a member of the senior management team – a thin, unsmiling woman. The lesson observation was a jumping-through-hoops ritual where people who don't teach watch you lecturing and pass judgement in order that you can progress up the pay-scale.

After my session, while I was waiting for the highest grade, Sally said to me, 'Aw, you don't want to worry about her, Jane. She's like a dry auld crispbread from the back of the cupboard.'

And she was right. All the money and the status and the title doesn't give you juice – doesn't give you *joie de vivre*. Isn't that something to aim for? Isn't that a valuable resource?

I think of the old lady and the vinegar bottle. Do you know the story? How she starts off in the vinegar bottle, and ultimately ends up back there, through a process of choices. I don't know if they're wrong choices or right choices, but the moral is, of course, to be happy with what you've got. I think about that as I'm pottering about here today – the idea of *striving* for something. Constantly striving. I think it is fair to say I've done a fair amount of that.

Has it got me what I want? Well, in part, and in a roundabout sort of way, yes – I am living in a beautiful house in an extraordinary spot. I sit here surrounded by many windows, all painted white with a view onto outcrops of pre-Cambrian rock in a Healthcliffian kind of way. There is a big sky. The mountain range in the east stretches all the way down from the Orme to Bardsey island, encompassing the Carneddau, yr Eifl, Tre'r Ceiri blue in the distance. The sound of birds. No people. Today I dropped Joe off at the beach with his friends, made some corrections to the design proofs and planted some fennel seeds. Nothing too taxing.

In another way, no; striving has not got me what I want, when it comes to Owning Your Own Home, and the implied security of that. That is what everybody is after, isn't it? But if I were to continue to strive, to really work myself against my natural inclination, with the aim of getting something 'better' later, wouldn't I simply be avoiding the very fulfilling things that are right under my nose, whether it is rented or not? The 'very fulfilling' things being gardening, gawping, writing, reading, walking. The energising things – the stuff that gives you life. The stuff that gives you staying power, stamina.

Does one actively drop the striving? Do you just give in to it – to life – trust that it will work out somehow, someday? Do you think rather that it *is* working out, that this is *it*? That, okay, you don't own your own home, but life is perhaps richer for it, in some unexpected way. Do you see things as they are *now*, right now, rather than planning for some future which you may not be able to realise or master?

At night I read books about Anglesey's history, flora and fauna. I read about Ordovician rocks and invasions – by English folk, Irish and Vikings. I wonder if I am descended from some of the Welsh families who ingratiated themselves with the English conquerors, in order to keep their land and favours. I wonder if they were smarmies, pragmatists, or rebels. Simple farmers perhaps.

The house is unusually quiet. James is in France, picking up the second batch of stuff: the kids are at Nana's. I am home alone, though Billy the partridge will be somewhere about – he likes to sit on the rock in the sunshine. There are quite a few rabbits around, some have droopy eyes and sad bodies. The postman thinks there may be myxomatosis about, or even that the gamekeeper has put something down, to scare away the rabbits and crows that might eat the partridges' eggs. The partridges will be shot by toffs in wellies some day soon. When I was putting out the bins two big brown rats shot out from behind them.

This evening, looking through old photos to choose some for my niece, Kizzy, I look at sundrenched French campsites, our old red Peugeot and a younger James sitting on the perimeter of our land. I remember how glad we were to sit on that patch when we found it, how we relished the peace and the big night sky. I think about how long ago that was and how we have changed, looking at gap-toothed photos of the kids. And I want to celebrate it, I am grateful for it.

I want to create a book that contains photographs of that journey, from the wide empty shots of the barn interior, clean and clear and full of distressed paintwork and plaster, through the higgle and shamble of the falling dutch barn outside, to the vans and trucks that we cleared away. So, actually, we did improve it, from the 'before' pictures with that scrabble of trucks and weeds and the 'for sale' pictures we put online which show that green swathe.

When I looked at those pictures of the barn recently it calmed me; the carmine rhododendron on the green grass, the memory of standing tall in the warm sun, perfectly self-contained, lean and upright.

Hardy

April 2013

The church is our nearest neighbour. We walk to it down a path which leads directly from the house, over a small stream, through a narrow gate and across the muddy field. It takes about two minutes. The church is set like the hub of a wheel, the spokes radiate from it to the outlying farms. There is only this house and one other down our track. The farm next door is a big place and usually empty, rented out to holidaymakers.

One evening in late September I was walking my usual circuit across the field after work. As I passed the church the windows were lit red and there was singing inside. I leaned against the wall for a while and just soaked it in. I started going to church. Nowadays the routine which at first seemed so complicated is more familiar to me, though I still sit at the back. The Welsh is fast and so intricate I stumble sometimes, but I've relaxed about that and now sometimes I just listen. There is a gravestone with my name on it, leaning to the left slightly. I don't know if this should unnerve me but it does not.

Sometimes in the evenings and mornings I do yoga. When I am balancing, I fix my gaze on a small tree I see out of the bedroom window and imagine the roots, going down.

One evening I got home from work late. I unloaded the car and brought in bags full of goodies for Joe's birthday. James said he'd had an 'unexpected visitor'.

'Jehovah's Witnesses,' I guess.

They've been here once before, with their shiny shoes.

'No.'

Another guess then: 'The Bishop of Bangor cathedral.'

No. I wouldn't have been surprised if it had been.

The visitor was my dad's older brother, accompanied by his cousin.

James describes how, as she walks into the house she says, 'Oh! It's changed!'

She goes straight to the back window of this house that she knows and points across to the farm next door. She tells James that my great-grandfather lived there and farmed this land.

I make James tell me again. I find myself crying as he does.

I walk out in the spring evening, over the bridge and around the golden field. I look back at the house in the fading light and imagine my forebears – forefathers – walking this land. Living here, dying here. Boots on lanes, familiar with this view. The mountains are so stark, snow on the peaks, like a parody of a great Western film. But real. Real like the windblown hawthorn, bent horizontal.

My limbs feel light and warm as I walk around the field. There is an overwhelming sense of peace. It is as though my paternal side – that element I have always missed – has moved in, like a great game of chess, with lives and choices and all the years. As though my taid, and great-taid, have seen my plight somewhere, something like that. Or maybe their wives, sisters and mothers.

Over the last few weeks I have discovered that my great-great grandmother was the daughter of the big house. She is buried in the church here: she was married in the church here. I can now trace my ancestors back even further, strong simple names that echo down the ages. From a lifetime of not really knowing who I was there is suddenly this strata of belonging, which is uncompromising, unequivocal in its truth and simplicity.

They are Welsh; they are religious. They are joiners, mariners and farmers. It's got so uncanny that sometimes I wonder if there's part of somebody else's spirit in me, that recognises these places. That is familiar with the lane, the trees, the primroses.

When I first saw the church I thought, with lightning surety: *I want to be buried there.*

It was an unspoken thing, a private clarity, clear as a bell. At the time, of course, I did not mention it – how do you mention something like that?

From not knowing of them, suddenly they are brought to life: Great-grandfather John's horse and cart going to market, down the track. Grandfather John leaving for the First World War and then returning. Suddenly there are a host of them, surrounding me, part of me, in this place.

Until now I did not know my father's family – my background was a complicated mass of loss and fragmentation. I knew my dad's father had died young, when my father was only a boy. I knew his family were 'farmers from Anglesey' – but that is all I knew. My grandfather and I never met, he was a bank manager in a coastal town. It just happens that his childhood was spent here, next door.

There have been patches of my life which have been very *unstable*, physically and psychically. In my youth I was a master of self-destruction. 'Anarchic', Simone called it. 'Boundary-less'. With a staggering lack of self-esteem I prostrated myself in all manner of unsuitable ways. I met two old friends recently, on separate occasions – people I hadn't seen for twenty-something years. They both expressed surprise that I was still alive.

Of course I put myself together over time. Some of the things I've written about here are part of that. What is astonishing, and what is still sinking in, is that this is where I come from, this is where I have landed. It gives me an immense feeling of solidity, that this is so. I now have a faded black and white photo of my great-grandparents, standing by the barn wall in the sunshine. It feels like home.

Acknowledgements

When Mary and John MacFarlan came to visit us in France, it was John who said 'You should keep a diary of this, Jane – how it really is'. He was kneeling on the cold concrete floor of the barn, building a rabbit hutch at the time – which is pretty indicative of how ace my parents-in-law are. I didn't tell them that I was doing just that. Writing my diary was an intuitive, necessary, stream-of-consciousness thing. I didn't set out to write it, and I didn't know then that it would make a book.

There are a lot of people in here whose names have changed but who I hope can recognise themselves, even in a brief sentence. That means you, Fletchers, Liz Ashworth, Mike Yates, Imogen Mowday, Carrie Canham, Sophie Tilley, Alison Mercer, Helen Jones, Louise Prendergast, Emrys Williams, Joel Cockrill, Peter Haveland, Dilomprizulike. Thanks to all my good friends for their wit and insight.

I'd like to thank Richard Davies at Parthian for his support and for making this project come to life. Thanks to Carly Holmes, for her expert editing, developing, trimming and tweaking.

Love always to my family – James, Joseph and Annabelle. Also, of course, to my ever-fabulous mother, for all things and everything – not least for the regular envoys of Red Cross parcels. Thanks Mum. To my dad, for being there when I needed him.

Coming back to Wales I found myself easily rooted. Bruce Parry, Maxie and Mairwen have shown me a whole new history. Diolch.

Quote from *Women who Run with the Wolves* by Clarissa Pinkola Estés. Published by Ebury. Reprinted by permission of The Random House Group Limited.

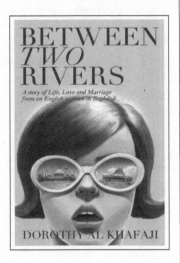